Saral Sarkar

Factors of Conflict and Conditions of Peace
An Essay

Dedicated to all peace-activists of the world

Saral Sarkar

Factors of **Conflict**
and
Conditions of **Peace**

An Essay

Table of Contents

Preface

In my school days, our textbook on the history of India appeared to me to be a series of stories of war and conquest by this king or that emperor. Even Ashoka the Great waged a merciless war against the king of Kalinga (in the 3rd century B.C.) before he felt remorse and became a Buddhist. Similar appeared to me to be the history of Great Britain, which we also had to read as school boys. Ever since, I have been trying to find – for myself only – the answer to the question *why there has been wars all through human history*.

Recently, I got a sort of answer from a story told by a famous modern historian in a TV broadcast: In 1522, in Rhodos, when the invasion army of the Sultan of Turkey had defeated the then ruling "Knights Hospitaller" and occupied the island, he ordered his soldiers to bring their Grand Master, a prisoner in their hands, to him. The Sultan said to him (in the general sense): Do not be sad. In this world kings and armies fight against one another, one army wins, and the other loses. That is the normal way of this world. (Christopher Clark in ZDF, Terra x)

Later, when I read more history, this impression from my school-days became stronger. A little reading on prehistoric archaeology was enough to see evidence of existence of war-like conflicts even before the dawn of civilization. Of course, in any part of the world, there has always been also shorter or longer periods of peace. But some or other kinds of conflicts – cold or hot – between large or small groups of humans were also always going on somewhere in the world.

Moreover, in times of absence of war, preparedness for war – with standing armies and reservists, and a certain degree of production and stockpiling of weapons – has always been deemed necessary. I have often heard or read about leading statesmen and politicians (e.g., Churchill and Kennedy) repeating a famous aphorism from the times of the Roman Empire: "If you want peace, be prepared for war."[1]

Also after the end of the World War II, there have been numerous conflicts that did sometimes end up in violent wars, e.g. the civil war in China in the second half of the 1940s and the Korean War in the 1950s. Generally speaking, conflicting parties have been living in a permanent state of alert and tension. Think of the long period of the Cold War between the two Super Powers. Oftentimes, conflicts are fought out by economic means, such as embargoes, boycotts, and sanctions.

In some Western European countries, there has been a tradition of peace movements, which began around the middle of the 19th century. When I came to West Germany in 1982, a big peace movement was going on there, which was engendered by the decision of the government of the country to deploy some of the latest kind of American middle-range precision nukes (called Pershing) aimed at the Soviet Union. The latter had earlier stationed similar nukes in Eastern Europe. Along with the whole Green Party,

I participated in that movement and had thereby opportunities to discuss with many peace activists the question of the basic factors of war and conflict.

They were all quite passionately active in the movement, were not only against any war, but also against any preparedness for war, which is why they were also "conscientious objectors" to compulsory military training/service. In the 1950s, their parents' generation had bitterly opposed the decision to found in the BRD a German army again, even though it was to be called the "Bundeswehr", suggesting that its mandate was only to defend their country by military means in case of a foreign invasion.

My discussions with such activists did not help me come any closer to an answer to the question I had in mind. In the second half of the 1990s, however, came for them the moment of truth. Many of the erstwhile radical peace activists, a large majority of whom were also members or voters of the Green Party, supported the decision of the SPD-Green coalition government to take part with its own air force in the NATO's bombing campaign against Serbia (1999). Cause? Around that time, Serbia was fighting against the armed Kosovar rebels' attempt to make their small province Kosovo independent of Serbia. Before that, no peace activist had ever imagined this could in some future become possible. So I decided to seek the answer to my question mainly through reading.

General and immediate motives and causes of (particular) past wars have all been studied and written about by scholar-historians. We know that, generally speaking, kings and emperors wanted to conquer new territories, for which they had to wage wars against other kings and emperors. Control over more territory was their main motive, because that was the precondition for more wealth: through tax revenue, tribute payments or through sheer plunder. Later, control of trade and trade routes became important, which is why in the late15th century, the Spaniards and the Portuguese searched for a sea route to India. Still later, desire to gain control over large markets and regions of production of coveted goods (in Asia) led to colonial wars, also between rival European powers. All these motives and causes can be clubbed together in the term *economic factors*, simply speaking, greed.

But there are also other, basic (for some, one could say, more basic) factors in play. To give here just one example, when, in the previous centuries, European settlers' colonies were founded in relatively sparsely populated, hitherto undeveloped regions/continents (America, Australia, Africa), the desire of large numbers of poor, even famine-stricken, people in relatively overpopulated European countries to start a new life also played an important role. For that purpose, they were also prepared to fight wars against indigenous peoples, as, for instance, the Dutch settler colonists in South Africa did against the resisting Zulus. Here, actually two factors were involved: economic and demographic.

It may also be that, in some exceptional cases, the spirit of adventure played the decisive role – e. g. in the case of Alexander the Great's invasive expedition deep into

Western India far away from his homeland Macedonia. In the case of the Pilgrim Fathers in the early 17th century, it was the spirit of freedom from religious persecution that was decisive.

In the pages that follow, I have mentioned and also written about these other factors, some of them very basic, as basic as the demographic and economic factors. They do not often come to mind of the average concerned people when they hear about some conflict, because they alone do not usually lead to wars or bloody fights. But they are basic factors nonetheless. They may remain unnoticed or barely noticed for a long time. But they may become manifest as causes of violent conflicts.

In this book I have presented a rather short version of what was originally planned to be a detailed study. It may prove to be a good decision. After all, one hears everywhere that in the age of internet and smartphone, would-be readers eschew detailed studies and are satisfied with short presentations.

I take this opportunity to state that I am not a scholar on any of the subjects dealt with here. I have been and am still an interested student of these subjects. I have read books, newspaper- and journal articles by scholars of these subjects. And I have continuously followed the international news in newspapers and TV news-broadcasts. Whenever I thought exact data are necessary, I have consulted the internet and Wikipedia. This essay is entirely based on knowledge thus acquired. I hope the average reader, particularly the average peace activist will find it interesting and/or useful.

Notes and References (Preface)

1. Publius Flavius Vegetius Renatus' Roman writer (4th or 5th century AD)

Editor's Preface

"Why war?" – this question has probably been on everyone's mind from time to time. In view of the almost unimaginable destruction and terrible human suffering that so often accompany wars, it would mean a genuine progress in human history, if wars could be consigned to the "dustbin of history". Moreover, the overwhelming majority of people – regardless of where they live - would certainly speak out clearly in favor of living in peace (if they were asked about it).

However, the current predominance in the media of reports on two wars of geopolitical dimensions is a painful daily reminder that we are in this respect still far removed from success in raising human development to a new level. Moreover, in recent years and decades, several smaller wars and armed conflicts have been going on in regions that seem to lie far away from us Western and Central Europeans.

So why do wars and violent conflicts stubbornly persist despite all the obvious atrocities that accompany them? And what are the conditions for peace to reign in and among human societies? Saral Sarkar explores these questions in this – quite long – essay in depth.

In March 2023, when I visited Saral, he told me that he had been working on a text on the topic of conflict and peace for quite some time and that he had originally planned it to be a relatively extensive book. He said he had already collected a large amount of material for this endeavor. But due to the limited energy and lifespan that he, as an old man, may still be left with, Saral decided to limit the volume of his work. At the time we met, he spoke of publishing a brochure. Now it has become a "real" book after all, albeit a slim one. However, the compactness of the presentation need not be a disadvantage, as Saral also points out in his foreword.

As both layout designer and editor, I only made minor changes to the text. They mainly involved checking and expanding the references, which made the sections on notes and references a little longer.

Many of the quotations in the text (mainly those from German) are translated by Saral himself. In some cases, however, the quotation is a translation done by Saral from the German language edition of the English original. Saral had to do this retranslation because it was not possible to access the English original (at least with reasonable effort). We apologize for any slight inaccuracies that may have resulted because of this procedure.

As we expect the book to be read in both English-speaking and German-speaking countries, some terms appear in both languages. We hope that we are using the correct terms.

Finally, I wish the reader an enjoyable and enlightening read. It is well worth it.

Ernst Schriefl
May 2024

Chapter 1

Introduction:
Aggression, Violence and War
among Homo sapiens

In ethology (behavioral science), the existence of intraspecific violence is seen as a part of normal behavior of animals. It is even regarded as necessary for, at least conducive to, the survival of a species. If, as is the practice among animals, only the strongest, the healthiest, and the cleverest of the males in a group mate with the females, then the progenies, that will form the next generation, can be expected to have a better chance of survival in the wilderness. For this to happen, however, the particular male must first fight off the rival males from within and outside the group and thus prevent the weak or sickly males from copulating with the females.

In carnivore animal groups, sometimes it also comes to half-violent quarrels over share of the meat of the slain prey. Sometimes even a mother-animal uses mild violence to compel her own grown-up brood-children to leave her territory and seek their own new foraging ground. Such intraspecific violence does not as a rule end in killing of a fellow member of the species, does not thus endanger the further existence of the group or the survival of the species. The weaker (defeated) male animal simply withdraws from the competition.

Konrad Lorenz (1963) calls such violence "the so-called evil". But he thinks, the so-called evil among animals developed into a real evil among humans, into an evil aggressive instinct. Among humans, it very often comes to intraspecific killing, even to murder, and to mass killings in wars. He *thinks* it came about in the thousands of years of the Paleolithic Age in the following way:

> „When man had reached the stage of having weapons, clothing and social organization, so overcoming the dangers of starving, freezing, and being eaten by wild animals, and these dangers ceased to be the essential factors influencing selection, an evil intra-specific selection must have set in. The factor influencing selection was now the wars waged between hostile neighboring tribes. These must have evolved into an extreme form of all those so-called 'warrior virtues' … "(Lorenz 1976: 34)

We see in the above quote that Lorenz assumes, even in earliest human history, the pre-existence of violence, even "war"[1] among enemy neighboring hordes.

But why should they have made war at all, two autonomous relatively big *groups* of humans fighting against one another? This view of Lorenz was strongly rejected by what we may call the *progressive or humanist camp*. They suspected Lorenz of serving the political interests of conservatives. Erich Fromm, a famous representative of this camp, wrote:

> „What could be more welcome to people, […] who fear themselves and feel themselves powerless to change the way of the world that is leading to destruction, than the

theory of Lorenz that violence comes from our animal nature and originates from an uncontrollable drive for aggression?" (Fromm 1974; quoted from Eibl-Eibesfeldt 1988/1997: 208., translated by S. Sarkar)

I find this kind of suspicion unfair. One did not blame Darwin for propounding the theory of evolution, even though his theory was misused by Social-Darwinists and racists.

However, Fromm also has some apparently cogent criticism of Lorenz's theory of origin of war. He argues as follows: Firstly, in view of the fact that in war, particularly in primitive warfare, very aggressive individuals are killed in large numbers, it is not plausible that hyper-aggression, as Fromm calls it, developed among humans by means of positive genetic selection through war. With the dead young warriors, the gene supposed to be responsible for such aggression should gradually disappear, leading actually to negative selection. The point Fromm is here trying to make is that such a gene does not exist, at least not anymore, if it had ever existed.

Secondly, Fromm argues further, before the advent of civilization, foragers (primitive hunters and gatherers) could not have much *economic motivation* to wage war. For population growth was negligible, there was not much moveable property that could be carried off, and slaves could not produce any surplus. Conflicts over hunting grounds or water holes were probably settled without battle. The stronger group (horde) just gradually pushed the weaker away.

I do not actually know whether Lorenz and ethologists of his school responded to Fromm's first objection, but I can imagine their response. They could respond by slightly revising their assertion, saying that such hyper-aggression is an innate drive and that it is present in every human male ever since humans evolved from our ancestral ape species. That is why the death of some particularly aggressive warriors cannot erase this drive from the human genome.

While we are at it, before proceeding further in the debate, let me present in short the aggression theories of Lorenz and Fromm.

Excursus (a): Aggression Theory of Lorenz (and his school)

Lorenz does not see behind aggression any interest-led drive. According to him, intra-specific aggression among animals is the result of an instinct that also exists among humans. But in this matter, there is a difference between animals and humans. Among animals, this aggression has a positive function for the survival of the species. It ensures that in the available habitat, individuals of the species are distributed at sufficient distance from one another; it guarantees selection of genetically better males (stronger, more capable of surviving), and it constructs a social hierarchical order that is useful in any group living. Aggression has fulfilled this function much better, ever since, in the evolution process, deadly aggression was transformed into symbolic and ritual threatening. Because of these positive functions, Lorenz calls the "evil" of aggression "the so-called evil" ("Das sogenannte Böse", the title of the German original, his main book).

Lorenz thinks that the human drive for aggression is fed by a continually flowing energy, which accumulates in the nerve center connected with this instinct. This leads to increase in pressure in a quasi-hydraulic system. For Lorenz, it is not only unhealthy to suppress aggression that wants to be released, it is also very difficult, if not impossible, to control it. When the pressure has risen too much, it can come to an explosion. Then a human being can become gruesome, murderous, even without a stimulus from outside. But as a rule, both humans and animals find some stimuli, they look for stimuli, or they themselves create stimuli. Lorenz gives the example of founding a political party, which generates stimuli, but is not really a cause of aggression.

Desmond Morris (1967/1994: 117) calls sports like wrestling, Judo, and boxing as "highly stylized versions" of "adult unarmed combat". I could add behaviour of groups of hooligan-fans of a soccer club who go to the stadium not so much to enjoy the match as to get an opportunity to fight against the hooligan-fan groups of the rival club.

Sometimes the release of pressure from spontaneously accumulating aggression takes place at the cost of inanimate objects. Lorenz wrote (somewhere) that he once found himself "attacking" a beer can lying on the street to release his aggression-pressure. This also happens when there is a provocation from some opponent. Violent demonstrators, who are provoked e.g., by a government decision, by employers, or the police, smash window panes of buildings, set fire to buses etc.

Morris (1967/1994: 109) writes:

> „What happens is that, because the object (the opponent) stimulating the attack is too frightening to be directly assaulted, the aggressive movements are released, but have to be re-directed towards some other, less intimidating object, such as a harmless bystander […] or even an inanimate object. […] When a wife smashes a vase to the floor, it is, of course really her husband's head that lies there broken into small pieces. It is interesting that chimpanzees and gorillas frequently perform their own version of this display, when they tear up, smash and throw around branches and vegetation."

Excursus (b): Erich Fromm's Theory of Aggression

Fromm – not an ethologist, but a social psychologist, who had a deep understanding of the human psyche (soul) and had studied the relevant literature in many fields – rejected (as shown above) the ethologists' aggression theory and presented his own, which can be summarized as follows:

Aggression is an instinct[2], which is nothing bad; it is even necessary. It is necessary for delimitation, self-assertion, and defense of one's vital interests, in short, for survival, and therefore it exists both in animals and humans. But, contrary to what Lorenz asserts, it is not an uncontrollable urge. It only comes into play as a *reaction* to threats (challenges) to one's *vital interests*. Fromm, therefore, speaks of *defensive or reactive aggression,* which is benign. Among animals, vital interests are the individual's own life, care for progeny, access to individuals of the opposite sex, access to sources of food, and survival of the species.

Among humans, however, vital interests can mean much more, which is why they can be more aggressive than animals. They can also react to foreseeable and imaginable future danger. They can create symbols, idols, and values, with which they identify themselves so much that an attack against or just a threat to them becomes an attack against or threat to one's vital interests. Finally, through education, ideology and brainwashing, all kinds of "vital interests" can be suggested to humans. But all these are not like those of animals, i.e. not innate among humans. They are results of the hitherto existing social structure based on exploitation and violence.

Fromm (1973: 185) writes:

> „If human aggression were more or less at the same level as that of other mammals, […] human society would be rather peaceful and nonviolent. But this is not so. Man's history is a record of extraordinary destructiveness and cruelty, and human aggression, it seems, far surpasses that of man's animal ancestors."

According to him "hyper-aggression" is unique to humans. What is unique to man is that he „can be driven by impulses to kill and to torture, and he feels lust in doing so; he is the only animal that can be a killer and destroyer of his own species without any rational gain, either biological or economic" (ibid: 218). Fromm calls this "sadistic-cruel destructiveness", also "malignant" aggression.

Unlike benign aggression, malignant aggression is a rare phenomenon in the animal world. Among humans, it is seen mainly as individual cases. It is a *pathological* form of reaction to human needs, i.e. it is not the result of an instinct common to all humans. Fromm explains it by the factor character, which is an individual matter. It is acquired and formed by external factors; hence, unlike an instinct, it can be changed by changing the external factors, namely social, economic and political structures.

Let us now come back to the debate. Contradicting Fromm's second argument, Irenaeus Eibl-Eibesfeldt (1984: 154), anthropologist and human ethologist, writes:

> „Sometimes it is argued that bellicose conflicts among primitive humans were improbable because, after all, in those times, not that many human groups lived on the earth. The argument is not well thought through. As we know, hunter-gatherers need very large territories, and, moreover, the conditions are not equally good everywhere. There are areas that are rich in game and plant foods, firewood and favorable waterholes, and there are areas that offer less favorable conditions of living. There is no reason at all to presume that our ancestors did not compete for the better living space. Archaeological evidence virtually proves that such competition was often also belligerent." (translated by S. Sarkar)

Fromm's argument that malignant aggression in humans is not an instinct, that it is only a matter of character, and can therefore be overcome by means of changes in our socio-economic structure is not very convincing. Those who believe in the existence of "evil" aggression in the human genome may point at the fact that primitive weapons – clubs, spears, bows and arrows – are very old inventions. Archaeologists date the oldest find of stone-tipped spear to 500 000 years ago. The oldest wood-tipped spear has been dated to 400 000 years ago. And not only humans, also chimps have been found to make wooden spears.[3]

And now, if we accept that conflicts over hunting grounds and water holes did exist (Fromm does not dispute that), the question logically arises, why shouldn't a numerically weaker horde try to defend its waterhole and hunting ground (both are vital interests) with weapons power against the attempt of a stronger horde to oust it from its *territorial possession*? Wild animals of almost all species do that with their weapons, namely with teeth and claws. Our nearest relatives in the animal world, the chimpanzees, also do that. In India, even city dogs – feral and often also those living in human families – do not generally tolerate the intrusion of alien dogs into their territory (unless it is a lonely bitch attractive enough for the local male dogs). Among humans too one can find examples of gang warfare over territory, e.g., in cities like Chicago, Los Angeles and London.

Not only among street gangs in cities, also among humans in general, a certain degree of resistance to too many foreigners coming in the town, city or the country as a whole (swamping) could actually be the effect of an innate dislike/fear of foreigners (or just of unknown persons). It is not only for economic reasons that there is a refugee problem in Europe today. When asked for the reason of their dislike, the resisting locals may advance some economic and/or cultural reasons. But human ethologists have observed this resistance even among small children, albeit in the form of fear.

Archaeological Evidence

Above, in connection with paleolithic weapons, we have already entered the realm of archaeological evidence. So let us now ask whether primitive human groups of the Stone Age used these weapons not only for hunting, but also for aggressive, violent acts of one group against another. We may now cite some evidence of the latter sort.

Eibl-Eibesfeldt, (1984: 151ff.), and Meller and Schefzik (2015), themselves archaeologists, cite numerous data from the works of earlier archaeologists who excavated and analyzed rests of skulls and other bones of humans from various periods of the Stone Age. The cited archaeologists had found that in all periods of the Stone Age humans killed humans, sometimes with stone axes, sometimes with arrowheads made of sharp stone pieces. That is evidence of deadly violence, but not in itself evidence of war in the Stone Age. However, they also found evidence of what could be called war between enemy human groups in rock paintings from the stone Age. These could not always be properly dated, but they all depict war between enemy groups of primitive people, in any case, groups of pre-civilization people. Some, however, could be dated back to the Paleolithic and Neolithic Age.

But why should primitive groups of humans have fought against each other at all? And how could many or most of the individual men of a horde be ready to form an attacking group? Let us try to answer the second question first. Morris (1967/1994: 118) calls this readiness "our undoing". He writes:

> „Aiding and abetting this mayhem is our specially evolved cooperativeness. When we *improved* this important trait in connection with hunting prey, it already existed in the animal world, e.g. among lions, wolves, wild dogs, chimpanzees etc. – it served us well, but it has now recoiled upon us. The strong urge towards *mutual assistance* to which it gave rise has become susceptible to powerful [emotional] arousal in intra-specific aggressive contexts. Loyalty on the hunt has become *loyalty in fighting*, and *war is born*. Ironically, it is the evolution of a *deep-seated* urge to help our *fellows*, loyalty to my ethnie, loyalty to my nation that has been among the main causes of all the major horrors of war. It is this that has driven us on and given us our *lethal gangs, mobs, hordes and armies*. Without it they would lack cohesion, and aggression would once again become 'personalized'." (italics by S. Sarkar)

But before loyalty in fighting could be demanded, there must be some cause for fighting. What were they in those days? We have above quoted Eibl-Eibesfeldt's reply to the question. Meller and Schefzik write: „A steeply rising density of population and climate change could have caused shortage of resources and, as a result of this, led to an Europe-wide crisis with warlike conflicts". (p. 105).

Also in connection with the archaeological find of Jebel Sahaba cemetery (Sudan, 13 000 years old), it has been noted that the warlike violence, if dated correctly, likely occurred in the wake of a local ecological crisis leading to shortage of resources[4].

Other reasons for violence between neighboring settlements could have been vengeance, demonstration of superiority, poaching in the neighboring group's territory, and kidnapping slaves.

If, however, anybody thought that the debate ended after all these strong evidence from archaeological sites, then he was mistaken. For even in 2013 Prof. Barash, an evolutionary biologist, regarded the emerging popular consensus about our „biological predisposition to warfare scientifically weak". He wrote: „Although there is considerable reason to think that at least some of our hominin ancestors engaged in warlike activities, there is also comparable evidence that others did not." He wrote further: „I seriously question the penchant of observers (scientific and lay alike) to generalize from small samples of […] our unquestionably diverse species," […] especially about something as complex as war (2013).

One important factor of prehistoric conflict and warfare must have been paucity of and fight for women. In the stone age, prehistorians logically assume, young women died in high numbers at child birth. So young men, they assume, also had to fight for women. After all, Fromm ranks „access to individuals of the opposite sex" among the vital interests of all animals, including humans. Such fights surely took place within a group, but often also between groups, which probably led to raids into another group's territory in order to get hold of the latter's women. Lawrence Keeley (1997: 86) writes:

> „Capture of women was one of the spoils of victory – and occasionally one of the primary aims of warfare – for many tribal warriors. In many societies, if the men lost a fight the women were subject to capture and forced incorporation into the captor's society. Most Indian tribes in western North America at least occasionally conducted raids to capture women."

Archaeological evidence, rather indications, of such a raid has for example been found in 1983 in the archaeological site of the "Talheim death pit" in Germany. Analyses of the skeletons found there suggest that prehistoric men from neighboring tribes were prepared to fight and kill each other in order to capture and secure women.

Some stories of abduction of women and near equivalents of that can also be found in ancient epics of civilized societies, e.g., *Ramayana* and *Mahabharata* of ancient India, and the *Iliad* of ancient Greece.

Parallels from Primatology

That chimpanzees are our closest relatives in the animal world is common scientific knowledge. About 99 percent of the genes of the two species are common. For this reason, Desmond Morris called humans *The Naked Ape* and Jared Diamond *The Third Chimpanzee*. Are there parallels in the behavior patterns of the two species? Can it be that both chimpanzees and Homo sapiens inherited from the long extinct ape-species from which they both evolved a genetic predisposition to intraspecific violence – killings and group attacks on other groups (hyper-aggression, war)?

Chimpanzees live in communities and smaller groups. Xenophobic animosity has been observed among groups belonging to different communities. They have a strong sense of territory. No group tolerates intrusion into its own by groups from a different community. That is why noisy clashes often take place at the borders. Such clashes are not just rituals, something also common among other species. Among chimps, they often degenerate into violence that demonstrates resolve.

However, it has also been observed that if a group of male chimps encounters a smaller group, they become murderous, particularly if they encounter a solitary individual from another community.

In the relevant literature there is a notorious case that was later interpreted as a *war* waged by one group of chimpanzees (Kalakase) against another (Kahame), the first observed case of this type. It was observed in 1974 by primatologists of the *Gombe Stream Research Centre* (Tanzania). They observed that the males of the Kalakase group crossed the border over to the territory of the other group, attacked a lone male member of the other who was enjoying a meal, and injured him so severely that he later died of his injuries. Chimpanzees are generally known to be very territory-conscious. So the crossing of the border and the attack was interpreted as deliberate.

To make the narrative shorter, it went on like this. In the course of three more years, one after another, all the other six grown up male members of the Kahame group were killed (i.e. they were severely beaten up and injured; thereafter, nobody saw them any more). By 1977, the Kahame group had ceased to exist (For details see Wrangham & Peterson 1996/2001). Similar observations have also been made in the Kibale National Park in Uganda (Meller et al. 2015) and at Mahale Mountains (Tanzania). After such "wars", the winners take over the vacant territory and the females of the defeated group.

The above are examples of war over territory. But killings have also been observed *within a community, even within a group*, as a result of power struggle. In such cases, a number of males gang up to kill a rival. It has also been observed that a strong female, aided by a male or another female, killed a weaker one's offspring.

Primatologist Frans de Waal comes to the conclusion that cimpanzees show tendencies toward group identification and that „there is no question that chimpanzees are xenophobic" (2006: 129, 133). Such observations among chimpanzees may lead us to believe that also primitive humans were such aggressive and xenophobic types and were prone to waging such "wars" against enemy human groups.

In my readings on this subject, I have noticed some confusion in use of the term "group". Authors have used two terms: a "community" can divide itself up into smaller "groups". It is not clear, whether the splitting is temporary or permanent, whether such groups, in course of time, feel themselves like different communities. According to all accounts of the "war" between the Kalakase and Kahame, the two groups were until a few years earlier members of the same "community", i.e. they were close relatives and friends. Yet, they *became* hostile groups. De Waal (2006: 135) writes:

> „[…] the phenomenon that emerged at Gombe involved chimps who actually knew each other. Over the years, one community split into a northern and southern *faction*, eventually becoming separate communities. […] These chimps had played and groomed together […] and lived in harmony. But the factions began to fight nonetheless. […] Not even the oldest community members were left alone. An extremely frail-looking male, Goliath, was pummeled for twenty minutes. […] Any association with the enemy was grounds for attack." (italics by S. Sarkar)

Similar developments have been described in the ancient Indian epic *Mahabharata*.

Social psychologists have carried out experiments among humans that show how quickly and easily new artificially built groups develop *new group identification*. In the experiments, the groups were randomly built from among people who were strangers or even knew each other well and/or formerly belonged to one and the same group (e.g., classmates). In the experiments, e.g. in a prison game, one group (guards) had to do things detrimental to the wellbeing of the other group (prisoners), or they (11 years old schoolboys) played during a summer vacation camp competitive games for trophies or honor. In the first experiment, they knew that they were only playing roles. and, in the second, the boys knew the vacation in the summer camp was short. Yet, they took their roles seriously, the artificially built groups soon became identity groups, and what had begun as an experiment or friendly matches became nasty. (For details, see de Waal 2006: 134; and Wrangham & Peterson 1996/2001). De Waal (2006: 134) comments: „Us-versus-them thinking comes remarkably easily to us."

The Noble Savage?

In the 1960s and 1970s, the perception of human nature was mainly based on anthropological (ethnological / ethnographic)[5] studies and observations of living primitive people made by Westerners till then. The ideology of the "noble savage" prevailed among scholars and intellectuals. Most popular and scholarly works written till the 1970s were influenced by and reflected this ideology. For example, Marshall Sahlins (1974: 30) quotes from Lejeune's report (1887) on the Montagnais (an Indian tribe of North America):

> „In the famine through which we passed, if my host took two, three, or four beavers, immediately, […] they

had a feast *for all neighboring savages*. And if those people
had captured something, they had one also at the same
time; […] I told them that they did not manage well, and
that it would be better to reserve these feasts for future
days, […] . They laughed at me. 'Tomorrow' (they said)
'we shall make another feast with what we shall capture'. Yes, but more often they capture cold and wind."
(italics by S. Sarkar)

E.R. Service (1966) whose book is the most comprehensive
presentation of anthropological/ethnological findings on
primitive hunters and gatherers, writes:

> „We are accustomed […] to think that human beings
> have a 'natural propensity to truck and barter and that
> economic relations […] are characterized by […] 'maxi-
> mizing' the result of effort, by 'selling dear and buying
> cheap'. Primitive peoples do none of these things, how-
> ever; in fact, most of the time it would seem that they do
> the opposite. They 'give things away', they admire ge-
> nerosity, they expect hospitality, they punish thrift as
> selfishness." (quoted in Fromm 1973: 138)

On the general evolution of society among primitive humans – in stark contrast to what Lorenz wrote in 1963 on
the evolution of warrior virtues among primitive people
through extremely positive selection, and also in contrast
to the conclusions of primatologists (see section above) –
Sahlins (1960) writes:

> „In selective adaptation to the perils of the Stone Age,
> human society overcame or subordinated such primate
> propensities as selfishness, indiscriminate sexuality,

dominance and brute competition. It substituted kinship and cooperation for conflict, placed solidarity over sex, morality over might. In its earliest days it accomplished the greatest reform in history, the overthrow of human primate nature, and thereby secured the evolutionary future of the species."

As to wars and warrior virtues, most authors of this period agreed that prehistoric warfare was rare, harmless, unimportant, and war is a disease of civilized societies alone. According to this view, primitive warfare was little more than a ritualized game, where casualties were limited and the effects of aggression relatively mild.

Thus, according to D. Pilbeam, there have of course been occasional feuds but no wars among primitive peoples. In such societies, wars have been nothing more than acts of revenge for alleged sorcery or long-drawn family feuds. Primitive groups never fight against each other. And it is difficult to imagine how a whole community could call its men together in order to defend its territory against another or why it should do that.

According to H. H. Turney-High, fear, anger and frustration are of course universal experiences. But the art of warfare developed late in human evolution. He thinks, most primitive societies were not capable of waging war, because that presupposes a high level of conceptualization. Most of them did not have a concept of organization that was necessary if one wanted to conquer a neighbouring territory. Most wars among primitive people were only armed scuffles and no wars at all (cf. Fromm 1994: 169f).

This noble-savage perception was gradually given up, changed or revised in the following decades, when more and more *archaeological excavations* of Stone Age sites were made. Summing up this development, Keeley (1997: 4f) writes:

„Even today, most views concerning prehistoric (and tribal) war and peace reflect two ancient and enduring myths: progress and the *golden age*. The myth of progress depicts the original state of mankind as ignorant, miserable, brutal, and violent. Any artificial complexities introduced by human invention or helpful gods have only served to increase human bliss, comfort, and peace, lifting humans out of their ugly and hurtful state of nature. The contradictory myth avers that civilized humans have fallen from grace – from a simple and primeval happiness, a peaceful golden age. All the accretions of progress merely multiply violence and suffering; civilization is the sorry condition that our sinfulness, greed, and technological hubris have earned us. In the modern period, these ancient mythic themes were elaborated by Hobbes and Rousseau into enduring philosophical attitudes toward primitive and prehistoric peoples.“

It all sounds like a matter of definition of different terms – feud, armed scuffle, battle, or war. Keeley (1997: 10) writes:

„Turney-High drew a very sharp line, literally a 'military horizon', above which *real warfare* was conducted by states and below which occurred only the *sub-*

military combat of primitives. He spoke of primitive warfare as being childish, 'reflecting the ways of human infancy' " (italics by S. Sarkar)

Be that as it may, the main point that is here relevant to our enquiry and that we should stress here is that these are all terms for *intergroup, not intra-group*, violent conflicts, that in fact existed among primitive people.

Eibl-Eibesfeldt, himself an anthropologist and ethologist (1984: 151f.), writes:

„The conception of a paradise, from which we humans were driven out, has also found acceptance in aggression research. A whole range of authors think that humans were originally peaceful. Striving for property and related conflicts arose only with the development of agri- and horticulture. Accordingly, cantankerousness does not belong to human nature. And this conclusion appears to reassure many people. We humans are after all not so bad. So everything would go well. Rousseau's thesis of peaceable primitive humans made a comeback in discussions on human nature." (translated by S. Sarkar)

Psychoanalytic Views

Up to here, I have presented and discussed theories of ethologists and their critiques. But much before Lorenz and his friends, Sigmund Freud and some other protagonists of what nowadays is often called "depth psychology" (*Tiefenpsychologie*)[6] have expressed similar views on these and similar matters.

In his famous letter to Albert Einstein, Freud (1933) wrote expressly of the existence of an aggression drive (*Aggressionstrieb / Destruktionstrieb*) in humans. Even Einstein, in his letter, to which Freud was replying, had wondered that it was so easy to enthuse people to start or join a war, and guessed that there was something that was working in them, a sort of a drive to hate and destroy. Freud fully agreed, and then elaborated the psychoanalytic theory of drives (*Trieblehre*).

He postulated two kinds of opposing drives: Eros (*Liebestrieb*), drives that work to keep the living being alive and unite and Thanatos (*Todestrieb*), drives that push the living toward death. In real life, the two kinds of drives work together, they amalgamate. Eros prevents Thanatos from being quickly successful. That is why the energy of Thanatos is turned outwards, it then comes to aggression against others instead of aggression against oneself[7].

Freud himself wrote in this letter that his theory of drives is actually only a theoretical apotheosis of the famous opposites loving and hating.

Also Alfred Adler – who originally belonged to the group around Freud, made himself independent and expressed original views on human nature – had, even before Freud, postulated the existence of an aggression drive as a basic drive in human nature. He saw in the First World War the result of excessive thirst for power (*Machtstreben*), and later in his life, he regarded any form of enmity and destructivity as an over- or wrong compensation for fear and feeling of inferiority. In the "Will to Power"

(*Wille zur Macht*) he saw only the deformation of a genuine human striving for perfection (cf. Rattner 1995: 28ff.)

Conclusion (of this chapter)

The purpose of this essay is not to try to come to some definitive *scientific* conclusion about aggression in humans. I simply am not qualified enough to do that. But it may be in order that I make some comments in conclusion of this chapter.

It is not possible to cite any direct concrete evidence to support the thesis of Lorenz. Whatever evidence one may cite from the world of today (or from written history) would necessarily come from the behavior of humans who live(d) in the period of civilization. The archaeological evidence cited here from the broader literature relate to humans who lived in the Stone Age. We know now that they waged "war", but we *do not know* what their motives were; we can only make intelligent guesses. Did they feel a sort of Lorenzian *"hydraulic pressure"* before starting an aggressive act against fellow humans (or inanimate objects)? We cannot ask them.

To draw conclusions about human nature on the basis of observations of animal behavior, as ethologists have done, does not help much, because one can easily dismiss them with the argument that humans are not just animals. August Kaiser writes (1973: 60–61):

> „A new born human is actually an animal that has only the possibility of becoming a human. Only in a field of contacts with fellow humans, it develops those needs

that characterize the human way of living. […] That means. the new born human baby must first *'learn to live'*
in the most comprehensive meaning of the phrase. […]
Essentially, it is dependent on what it is taught. In its
enormous weakness and helplessness, it needs great
care and intensive love in order to be able at all to gain
a foothold in life." (italics by S. Sarkar)

This „becoming a *social* human" is a delicate and very
trouble-prone process. Social behavior in later life gets
here its *decisive* form (ibid. 60 – 61). So, for such behavior
it is not one's general genetic endowment that is decisive.

If we now decide to limit our thoughts on aggression to
humans who live(d) in and under the influence of civilization, then much speaks for the theses of Fromm and the
"progressives". But the age of civilization is just about 5
thousand years long. And species of the genus Homo are
living on the planet since about 2 million years ago[8].
Equally old are most of the genes that make humans. *Modern* humans are, of course, products of culture, but they
are an ape species nonetheless. Are we also going to dispute the science of genetics or the theory of evolution? The
presence of evil aggression (Lorenz) or hyper-aggression
(as Fromm calls it) among chimpanzees, our nearest relatives, should be taken as a pointer to a part of our own
nature. Morris (1967/94) advised us already in the 1960s to
„take a long hard look at ourselves as *biological specimens*
and gain some understanding of our *limitations*. […] It
helps to *keep a sense of proportion* and to force us to consider
what is going on just below the surface of our lives." (italics by S. Sarkar). He further advised us: „You are a

member of the most *extraordinary animal species* that has ever lived. Understand your *animal nature* and accept it" (Morris 1994: Introduction to the reprint, italics by S. Sarkar).

In almost the same vein Edward O. Wilson, biologist and chief protagonist of sociobiology, wrote:

„Chimpanzees are close enough to ourselves in the details of their social life and mental properties to rank as nearly human in certain domains where it was once considered inappropriate to make comparisons at all. These facts are in accord with the hypothesis that human social behavior rests on a genetic foundation – that human behavior is, to be more precise, organized by some genes that are shared with closely related species and others that are unique to the human species. The same facts are unfavorable for the competing hypothesis which has dominated the social sciences for generations, that mankind has escaped its own genes to the extent of being entirely culture-bound." (1978/1995: 32)

The best conclusion for this chapter, I think, would be a quote from human-ethologist Eibl-Eibesfeldt (1990: 81). He writes:

„Our innate characteristics are not laid down for ever. We are capable of controlling our nature through our culture. However, *we must first have a good knowledge about ourselves*. What is decisive is that we humans are the first creatures to be in a position to set goals for us and thereby give a meaning to our life. That *does not mean that we cease to be a part of nature*, but we actively put ourselves in new situations, in which new conditions of selection affect us." (translation and italics by S. Sarkar)

Here I have only one more comment: When ethologists use the term "selection", they generally mean genetic selection. My question is: Can adaptation to new situations come about through a learning process, i.e. through culture? The answer is: Yes. But can such successful adaptations become *ingrained*? As if replying to my question, Wilson writes:

> „When societies are viewed strictly as populations, the relationship between culture and heredity can be defined more precisely. Human social evolution proceeds along a dual track of inheritance: cultural and biological. Cultural evolution is Lamarckian and very fast, whereas biological evolution is Darwinian and usually very slow." (1978/99: 78)

Further down, Wilson writes:

> „Yet the divergence cannot become too great, because ultimately the social environment created by cultural evolution will be tracked by biological natural selection. […] I do not for a moment ascribe the relative performances of modern societies to genetic differences, but […] there is a limit, […] beyond which biological evolution will begin to pull cultural evolution back to itself." (ibid. 79 – 80)

That may be the ultimate explanation for the anomalous phenomena that we humans have been trying for more than a century now to bring about lasting global peace, but are seeing even today several conflicts and wars in many parts of the world.

Notes and References (Chapter 1)

1. In recent times, war has been defined by scholars of the subject as follows:

„War is a planned and organized armed encounter between autonomous groups. Violence between individuals or factions within a local group does not fall under this category, also not feuds and blood vendettas. A further essential aspect of war is that violence is accepted as legitimate by at least one of the parties, so that killing is allowed in war without being branded as murder." (Meller and Schefzik: 2015:11; translated from German by S. Sarkar).

2. *Instincts* are goal-directed and innate *patterns of behavior* that are not the result of learning or experience. A *drive* is an instinctual *need* that has the power of driving the behavior of an individual; an „excitatory state produced by a homeostatic disturbance" (from the internet).

3. „The oldest stone tips, the interpretation of which as arrow tips is however disputed, were found in Abri Sibudu (Province KwaZulu-Natal, South Africa) and are about 64 000 years old. Earliest find outside Africa (Sri Lanka) ~48 000 years ago. In Europe, flint tips with stems, which were probably arrow tips, exist since […] 22 000 to 18 000 BCE. They can be interpreted as the oldest indirect proof of existence of bows." (https://de.wikipedia.org/wiki/Bogen_(Waffe), accessed: 15.4.2024, translated by S. Sarkar)

„Spear manufacture and use is not confined to humans. It is also practiced by the western chimpanzee. Chimpanzees near

Kédougou, Senegal, have been observed to create spears by breaking straight limbs off trees, stripping them of their bark and side branches, and sharpening one end with their teeth. They then used the weapons to hunt galagos sleeping in hollows." (Information and quote from https://en.wikipedia.org/wiki/Spear, accessed: 7.4.2024)

4. https://en.wikipedia.org/wiki/Jebel_Sahaba (accessed: 6.4.2024). Quoted from there: „Hoffman (1993) argued that the conflict took place due to climate change. By the late paleolithic, the Qadan culture had developed crop harvesting, being among the first cultures to do so. However, climate change reduced crop yields, and the resulting lack of resources would have given an incentive for local social groups to compete for resources through violent struggles such as at Jebel Sahaba. Hoffman's thesis has not been contested. Decades later, a 2021 study stated that "major climatic and environmental changes" remained the most probable explanation."

5. *Ethnology, Anthropology* (difference)
Ethnology and Anthropology are two disciplines between which some difference can be observed. First, let us define the two words. Anthropology is a field of study that focuses on human origins, societies, and cultures. On the other hand, ethnology is the study of the characteristics of different peoples. The key difference between anthropology and ethnology is that while anthropology can be viewed as an overarching field of study, ethnology is only a subfield of it.

6. In this subchapter the German original terms (as used by Freud and others) are put in brackets, like aggression drive (German: Aggressionstrieb / Destruktionstrieb), and others.

7. https://www.spektrum.de/lexikon/psychologie/todestrieb/15627 (accessed: 6.4.2024)

8. The two oldest species of the genus Homo are Homo rudolfensis and Homo habilis, which lived around 2.5 to 1.5 million years ago (https://de.wikipedia.org/wiki/Homo, accessed: 15.4.2024). "Modern" humans (species Homo sapiens) have existed for about 300 000 years, as documented by fossil finds (https://de.wikipedia.org/wiki/Mensch, accessed: 15.4.2024).

Chapter 2

Scarcity, Limits to Growth, Limits to Resources

In chapter 1, section on archaeological evidence, we have referred to the opinion of some archaeologists that also in the stone age, primitive foraging people (hunter-gatherers) did at least occasionally suffer from material scarcity and poverty – due perhaps to population growth or vagaries of climate and weather causing droughts and floods or a combination of both. The question is only how they behaved in such situations. Did they perpetrate violent attacks on (waged "war" against) the neighboring group of people who probably had enough and try to rob them? Or did the latter share whatever food and water they had with the suffering neighbors? Based on the evidence they saw, archaeologists concluded that "war" was at least not so uncommon in such situations of dire poverty or even hunger.

We have also seen (ch. 1) that Erich Fromm and many anthropologists and ethnologists of the 19th and early 20th century concluded from what they observed among primitive people of their times that the latter were, generally speaking, generous, cooperative, spendthrift even in times of famine, and not so bellicose as many of their contemporaries imagined.

We know that in today's world – in fact since the beginning of civilization, if not already since the Neolithic revolution, when farmers began a sedentary life – humans, generally speaking, are rather the opposite of what Fromm and other writers of his ilk think about the character of primitive people. Most of us think, humans are and have always been, in general, selfish, greedy, acquisitive, and ready to defend their property and special rights, if need be, by violent means.

It is a question whether primitive people generally lived in a state of material scarcity and whether for that reason they had to toil hard to sustain themselves. The hunter-gatherers Marshall Sahlins (1974: chapter 1) wrote about worked only three to four hours a day. But why not more? Were they satisfied with their degree of material "affluence"? As if in reply to this question, Sahlins (1974: 1-2) writes in a paper entitled "The Original Affluent Society":

„For there are two possible courses to affluence. Wants may be 'easily satisfied' either by producing much or desiring little. […] But there is also a Zen road to affluence, departing from premises somewhat different from our own: that human material wants are finite and few, and technical means unchanging but on the whole adequate. Adopting the Zen strategy, a people can enjoy unparalleled material plenty – with a low standard of living."

Needs and Wants of the Modern Human Population

We know that as a whole, we modern humans of the 3000 to 4000 years long Age of Civilization are trying to easily satisfy our wants by producing much rather than by desiring little. This is the course to affluence that already our forefathers who became the first Neolithic farmers chose to follow. In the past, there have of course been a few ascetic monks and sages, who followed the other course, that of desiring little. But they have always been a miniscule minority. And today, hardly anybody among us subscribes to the Zen strategy mentioned by Sahlins, not even monks in cloisters.

But it may also have been that the pressure of a slowly growing population gradually also *compelled* our forefathers to produce ever more. In that case, they hardly produced any affluence. And if they succeeded in producing more, but just enough to satisfy the bare material wants of their growing numbers, then they hardly achieved it "easily"

Demography historians have presented their estimates of human population growth in a diagram. It shows that the world population has been growing continuously and exponentially since the Neolithic Revolution (New Stone Age) some 10 thousand years ago[1].

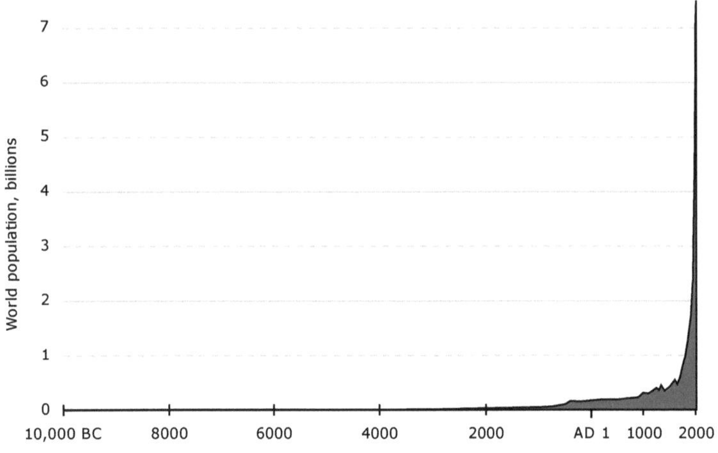

Figure 1: World population from 10,000 BC to 2000 AD. Source: https://en.wikipedia.org/wiki/Estimates_of_historical_world_population (accessed: 13.4.2024), Public Domain

Let us take just a few numbers from our times:

In 1960 global human population was 3 billion,

in 1974   4 billion

in 1987   5 billion

in 1999   6 billion

in 2011   7 billion

(Data from Schriefl 2021: 60).

And now, at the time of writing (2024), it is over 8 billion.

Parallel to population growth, some other processes have been taking place in the human world as a whole, but also in every individual country, more or less.

Chimpanzees, primatologists tell us, invented hammer and ambos for cracking nuts and crafted thin twigs into tools for angling eatable ants out of anthills. Among humans, the process of inventing and making tools went on continuously, far beyond such a simple level, and ever faster. As a result, producing the basic necessities of life indeed became ever easier. Ever better and ever more tools enabled us to produce a surplus which, inter alia, had the effect that less and less people died of hunger and human population started growing faster than before.

Necessity, i.e. hunger, had been the mother of invention, as the saying goes. But in the following centuries and millennia the original spirit of inventing tools gathered momentum, developed its own dynamics. And it increasingly aimed at producing better weapons of war, and satisfying new "needs" and wants that human imagination itself created. A Marxist would say: *basic* needs are co-related to the level of development of the productive forces. Otto Ullrich (1979: 108) expressed it succinctly, but critically, and in a different context:

> „In a system that tries to satisfy needs through material production […] there will always be for every level of 'material wellbeing' some new unfulfilled basic material needs, above all because this system is necessarily very inventive in the production of new luxury goods, which soon become the models of new basic material needs. This system will always be too poor […]. What was the day before yesterday the radio, was yesterday the black-and-white TV, is today the color TV; and tomorrow it will be the 3-dimensional picture projector."
> (translated by S. Sarkar)

All kinds of leftists will blame this "system" on capitalism and its efforts to create new needs by means of advertisement. But it was a Greek mythology writer who imagined Ikarus und Daedalus flying like birds, and it was Jules Verne who imagined a journey to the moon. None of them was a capitalist.

Limits to Growth

The concurrency of population growth and productivity growth achieved through ever more use of ever better tools and by other means such as irrigation, use of manures and the three-field system had its limit. When this limit was reached, population growth had to lead to extensive agriculture: more and more land under the plough, more and more cattle in the stable, increasing deforestation, use of marginal land, emigration to still sparsely populated countries, and finally, conquering new continents and colonialism. The surplus populations of Europe were accommodated in the conquered continents, which were by no means *terrae nullius* (nobody's land, unpopulated land), by killing off, partly also through imported diseases, or pushing away the indigenous populations to more and more inhospitable bad lands. All that is known history.

Even for the Crusades, allegedly a military expedition to wrest the holy city of Jerusalem from Muslim reign, overpopulation in Europe was, according to historians, an important causal factor. The umpteen supernumerary younger sons of the European nobility were of course knights, but they neither had any chance under the prevailing inheritance laws to possess their own estate nor wanted to become a monk or priest. They saw in the crusades an opportunity to have their own estate. It is they who assumed the leadership in the expeditions. And the excess rural population also followed them as foot soldiers, accompanied by their whole families as hangers-on, in order to have a chance to escape poverty at home.

Historian Robert Bartlett confirms this interpretation of the Crusades: In the 11th century – due to favorable climatic conditions and new developments in agricultural technology – there had been a population explosion in some European countries. This also led to an expansion in the peripheries of Europe[2].

This was partly also the case during the Iberian conquest of South America. Younger sons of the nobility and young people from the poor underclass took the initiative in colonizing the American continent.

Malthus Was Not Wrong

Malthus was the first economist who theorized – in my opinion, convincingly – on the population problem. But he has been much reviled by all kinds of leftists, feminists, Marx and Engels themselves, and more recently, also by many people who claim to be ecologists or environmentalists. He has been dismissed as a conservative, and, what is worse, as a spokesperson and lobbyist of the bourgeoisie and landed aristocracy. He has been most reviled for a passage in the original first edition of his essay, which he felt compelled to delete in the subsequent editions of his book. It reads as follows:

"A man who is born into a world already possessed, if he cannot get subsistence from his parents on whom he has a just demand, and if the society does not want his labour, has no claim of *right* to the smallest portion of food, and, in fact, has no business to be where he is. At Nature's mighty feast there is no vacant cover for him. She tells him to be gone." (quoted in Gide et al. 1953: 140-141, italics by S. Sarkar)

Malthus added that Nature does not fail to bring even this command to execution.

I am not shocked at these words of Malthus. They are telling the truth. Even in the 1950s to the 1970s, I have come across many such hungry men and women in India, who, in fact, had literally the least right to demand any portion of food. Of course, they had a *moral* right, because, after all it is not they who wanted to be born. It is their parents who brought them into the already occupied world. They were prepared to give their labor in exchange for food. But neither their parents nor the society at large could meet this moral demand. Many of course did not care, and many pretended as if they just did not see.

Anybody who does not turn his back and is willing to see, can see the hundreds of thousands of hungry, expelled or fleeing refugees from the drought-, war-, and violence-stricken regions of Africa, the Middle East, Central America, South Asia etc., who are thronging the refugee camps set up in the neighboring countries. Millions of others – unemployed young men and women from such countries, people without a perspective – who are willing to work in exchange for a better life, are sacrificing their dignity and very often even risking their life while trying to illegally cross the borders to Europe and North America.

To understand and appreciate Malthus's population law, we must first quote the law and then interpret it. It says: „Population, when unchecked, increases in a geometrical ratio [exponentially]. Subsistence increases only in an arithmetical ratio." (quoted in Catton 1980: 126). In his book, when he said "population", Malthus always meant human population, and when he said "subsistence", he meant food. But, in William Catton's (1980: 126) opinion

> „[…] the really basic Malthusian principle is so important that it needs to be restated in the more accurate vocabulary of modern ecology. It states a relationship of inequality between two variables: The cumulative biotic potential of the human species exceeds the carrying capacity of its habitat." (ibid.)

Malthus also uses the words "when unchecked", with which he means to say *potentially*. We know that in a natural environment, nature sees to it that every generation of any species of living beings including humans can/does produce offspring (or seeds) at a rate much higher than the replacement rate. The surplus is, one may almost say, *meant to be* devoured/eaten away by the respective predator species or cannot survive because of various other reasons – processes that act as *checks* to the numerical growth of the prey species. As for humans, we know that there are still countries, where the human population is growing very rapidly because there the checks to growth are very weak or even nonexistent. And there are countries where the human population is decreasing because the indirect checks there, e.g. high cost of better living, are too many or too strong.

We modern humans have succeeded – thanks to our intelligence, sophisticated tools and weapons power – in subduing and reducing, though not eliminating, all current and potential predators and dangers. In this we succeeded so well that now we have even to save some species that could potentially harm us – the tiger, the wolf and the lion, for example. However, apart from natural death and some acts of nature beyond our control (earthquakes, epidemics of incurable diseases etc.), there are dangers and causes of decimation that we humans ourselves have given rise to. These are the checks, though very weak, that are till now keeping our population from growing faster.

Foremost among them are wars of all kinds. Then come environmental pollution and global warming leading to climate catastrophes. These are the best-known and most acknowledged as past and potential causes of our decimation. Thus, e.g., it is estimated that in the 30-Years War (1618- 1648), the population of Central Europe – in what was then called the Holy Roman Empire – was decimated to an extent of about 45 percent. Other estimates speak of 8 million deaths in a total population of 16 million. And today, many scientists fear that global warming, climate change, environmental pollution and biodiversity loss may make the planet uninhabitable for humans.[3]

Rwanda – Genocide – a Malthusian worst case

How right Malthus was and how much population has still to do with decimation of human numbers can be best illustrated with the case of the Hutu-Tutsi conflict in Rwanda, that culminated in 1994 in the genocidal killing of ca. 800 000 (mostly) Tutsi perpetrated by the Hutu. I do not here want to narrate the whole story of that genocide. That has been done by many competent authors.[4] Instead, I shall only highlight the facts and figures that are relevant to my contention.

In 1993, Rwanda's population of 6.84 million was growing at the rate of 3.1 percent per annum. They were living on a total area of 26,338 square Kilometer. With 260 people per square kilometer, the country had one of the highest population densities in the world. Fertility rate in 1993 was 6.5 births per woman.[5]

Rwanda's fertile land, adequate rainfall, and mild climate are quite favorable to agricultural growth. The altitude at which the country was situated kept malaria away. Yet, the advantages from all these favorable circumstances were nullified by the high rate of population growth. In 1990, about 94 percent of the population lived in rural areas. And most of them had to live off farming. Opportunities for off-farm income through professions such as carpentry were few.

Because of the high population density, farm-sizes were small to very small. The few big farms were called so because they measured more than 1 to 2 acres. Agricultural productivity was low because of absence of mechanization and other modern methods of farming. To give an example, in the hilly country, farmers ploughed their land up and down, apparently ignoring the advantages of terrace cultivation.

When, in the 1960s and again in 1973, many Tutsi were killed or fled the country, and their land was taken over by the Hutu, per capita food availability increased. Many Hutu farmers thought then that they now had enough land to feed their families. But after 1981, it again gradually fell back to the 1960s level. It had to fall because in these 20 years the population had not ceased to grow.

Family planning was not unknown in Rwanda. There was even an office or department of family planning. But it was good for nothing. It was mainly created to enable foreign donor agencies to give Rwanda development aid. Also the negative influence of the Catholic Church was too strong.

Jared Diamond quotes Gerard Prunier, a scholar of East Africa:

> „[…] part of the reason why it [the genocidal killing] was carried out so thoroughly by the ordinary rank-and-file peasants in their ingo [= family compound] was the feeling that there were too many people on too little land, and that with a reduction in their numbers, there would be more for the survivors." (Diamond 2006: 326).

Diamond also quotes two other observers, André and Platteau:

> „The 1994 events provided a unique opportunity to settle scores, or to reshuffle land properties, even among Hutu villagers. […] It is not rare, even today, to hear

Rwandans argue that a war is necessary to wipe out an excess of population and to bring numbers into line with the available land resources." (ibid: 326)

Let us now come to the end of this part of the story. After 1994, many outside observers had thought that the genocide was the result, the tragic culmination of a decades-long hateful power struggle between the two ethnic groups Hutu and Tutsi. That this power struggle, this hatred, existed cannot be denied. (I shall come back to this point in the next chapter). These were facts. Fact was also that after the Hutu took over power, there emerged different factions among them who competed for dominance. But the Hutu-Tutsi ethnic conflict need not have been resolved through such a barbaric genocide. I find the conclusion arrived at by Jared Diamond convincing. He writes:

„I am accustomed to thinking of population pressure, human environmental impacts, and drought as ultimate causes, which make people chronically desperate and are like the gun powder inside the powder keg. One also needs a proximate cause: a match to light the keg. In most areas of Rwanda, that match was ethnic hatred whipped up by politicians cynically concerned with keeping themselves in power." (ibid: 326)

The Israel-vs.-Palestine conflict

Since October 2023, we are witnessing the Israel–Hamas war in Gaza. Here too, many people first think of ethnic or religious hatred as the cause of the long-drawn conflict.

Some people also speak of an anti-colonial liberation war being carried out by the Palestinians.

These points are of course partly true. But what most observers and commentators leave unmentioned is the deeper cause of the intractability of the conflict: that it is a *war over birthrates*. As soon as I opened the internet and searched for the population growth rate of the two ethnic groups, I found the following lines: Let me quote them verbatim:

> „The estimated Palestinian world population has increased 10-fold since the Nakba from 1.37 million in 1948 to an estimated 14.3 million by mid-2022, some 7.1 million of them inside historic Palestine, representing 49.9% of the total population (Israelis and Palestinians).“[6]

The population of Israel is also growing?

> „In this war over birthrates, it may seem like good news for Israel that by 2040, the country's overall population is projected to increase by another two million people, reaching 12 million. However, the Jewish population is growing mostly thanks to one community, the haredim, or the ultra-Orthodox.“[7]

That means there is no solution until and unless the population of both the population groups stops growing. Because land and resources available in Palestine are limited.

Notes and References (Chapter 2)

1. In roughly the first 10 millenia after the Neolithic Revolution (dated about 10,000 BC), the human population was growing very slowly. If, during these times, it had been growing exponentially at all, then at a very low growth rate.

2. https://de.wikipedia.org/wiki/Kreuzzug (accessed: 13.4.2024), Bartlett (1993).

3. According to David Wallace-Wells (2019) who interviewed many high level scientists working on the subject of climate change and environmental pollution.

4. See e.g., Diessenbacher (1998), Diamond (2006)

5. Daten der Weltbank, https://data.worldbank.org/indicator/SP.DYN.TFRT.IN?locations=RW (accessed: 13.4.2024)

6. Palestinian Academic Society for the Study of International Affairs, Factsheet Population, http://passia.org/media/filer_public/50/f1/50f1cdf6-42d6-430c-b5bc-1078b7ce5845/factheet_population.pdf (accessed: 24.4.2024)

7. https://aspeniaonline.it/israel-a-demographic-ticking-bomb-in-todays-one-state-reality/ (accessed: 14.4.2024)

Chapter 3

Quasi Species of Homo Sapiens

In Rwanda, the conflict between Hutu and Tutsi had simmered for quite some time before it exploded into the genocidal killing spree in 1994. We have also seen that the ultimate cause of the conflict was continuously declining per capita availability of fertile land, the most essential resource, due to exponential population growth.

A foreigner coming for the first time to Rwanda or Burundi, where too these two ethnic groups live and compete for power, may not at first see any physical difference between them. But a closer look will reveal some minor ones. All original Africans are of course dark-skinned, but „it is often stated [and TV documentary reports roughly confirm – S. Sarkar] that the two groups look different, Hutu being on the average shorter, stockier, darker, flat-nosed, thick-lipped and square-jawed, while Tutsi are taller, more slender, paler-skinned, thin-lipped and narrow chinned" (Diamond 2006: 314).

One can *see* that Mr. Kagame, the current President of the country, is a Tutsi. Idealists (want to) tell a different story: A group of European paleoanthropologists had done some excavations in South Africa and found some very old (fossilized?) bones of ancient humans. Bishop Desmond Tutu, Nobel Peace Laureate, who was sojourning nearby, dropped in to see their work. He asked them, in the general sense: What do the bones say? A scientist replied: These humans were among the very original inhabitants of Africa. „And we?", asked Bishop Tutu, „are we also original Africans?" The scientist replied: „All people everywhere are originally African." (He meant of course Homo Sapiens, who originated in Africa). Tutu burst out into his characteristic loud laughter and said: „Isn't it great to hear that all humans are Africans?" (seen/heard in a TV documentary).

Or take these words, which I heard in Germany at a political event against xenophobia: A participant, a German activist, said in her intervention: „All humans are foreigners, *almost* everywhere." Or this one: „No Racism! Only one race: the human race!" (Slogan on a placard in an Anti-Trump demo).

This idealist attitude stands in stark contrast to the realities of this world. To be effective, peace activists must first take cognizance of the unpleasant realities of life.

Race, Quasi Species, Racism

Professor of sociology Karin Priester (2003: 6) writes in her book on racism that already her predecessors in this branch of science regarded *race* to be an analytically useless concept. She informs us that already in 1935, the famous biologist Julian Huxley and anthropologist Alfred Haddon demanded that the use of the term race for groups of humans should be banished from the vocabulary of science, because it is too vague, too indistinct, and too imprecise. At the latest, after the end of the Second World

War, it is no longer being used by the scientific community.

The term *race* may have been banished from the vocabulary of science, but it is thriving as ever – in popular language and especially in the related derived term *racism*. For instance, in the popular slogan „No Racism! Only one race: the human race" quoted above, the phrase "the human race" is wrong. The author should have said "the human species". And instead of saying "No racism!", s/he should have said "No discrimination!"

Pseudo Species or Quasi Species

Ethologist Irenäus Eibl-Eibesfeldt (1984: 37 ff.) maintains that the human species, though biologically one, is *factually* divided into many *pseudo species,* that come up through the process of *"cultural" development*. He calls the process "pseudo speciation". And ecologist William Catton (1980: 104 ff.) speaks of *quasi species,* that come up through extensive differentiation on social and occupational lines (the process is then called "quasi speciation").

I think it is better to use the term *quasi species,* used by Catton, because the differences between the "pseudo species" are not at all pseudo differences; they are very real (e.g., religious differences) and are often clearly perceptible. One also reads of the existence of *subspecies*. But the use of this term is restricted to indicate only biological/physiological/morphological differences. The term *quasi species*, in contrast, is also amenable to use in case of differentiation through cultural development and can be used to indicate the existence of *many kinds* of non-biological differences within the human species – differences that form bases of group-building in human societies, groups that may have or may develop conflicting interests in the same society or state.

The significance of using the term quasi *species* (instead of simply *group*) in this sense lies in the fact that it indicates that humans – like predator and prey species in the animal kingdom – can and do kill members of other human groups, who actually all belong to the same species, when that serves their interest. The worst case is a genocide. Examples of milder alternatives to killing are enslavement of other peoples (Blacks of Africa) or colonial conquest of other peoples' land and/or their complete displacement. In chapter 1, we have seen the existence of a similar phenomenon among chimpanzees, our nearest relatives in nature.

Recognizing the real existence of such quasi species, of differences among them and their material interests, and resolving the conflicts arising from such interests are very important for achieving peace within a state as well as in the global human society.

Such differences are those based on or relating to physical appearance (often still called "racial"), sex, sexual orientation, language, religion (philosophy of life: e.g., theist or atheist), territoriality, culture in the anthropological/ethnological sense – i.e., behavior patterns, customs and traditions, traditional laws, mythology, clothing, housing, food/cooking etc. – and also culture in the sense of the fine arts (music, dance, drama etc.). Differences based on such things are often identity-giving – i.e., if not super-seded by a higher identity-giving fact, e.g., being a European or Asian, or South Asian. (Samuel Huntington (2004) has written a whole book on this subject). However, in the recent history of the world, we have seen cases, in which even the existence of a legally-constitutionally sanctified higher identity like citizenship of the same state could not supersede an identity of a lower order, such as, racial, religious or linguistic.

Race or Ethnie?

The term *race* could be and indeed has been to a large extent replaced by the term *ethnic group* (or *ethnie*)[1]. In the above quote from Diamond, we see that the author is referring to the physiognomic differences, albeit slight, between the Hutu and the Tutsi. But they are called ethnic groups, not races. It is also right to do so, because, as Diamond (2006: 314) shows, the main points of difference that led to the violent conflicts between the Hutu and the Tutsi were not the physiognomic differences, but, firstly, the fact that the Hutu were mainly small farmers, whereas the Tutsi were originally mainly herders. And, secondly, the fact that the Tutsi „established themselves as the overlords over the Hutu" (Diamond 2006: 314). When the European colonial powers (first the Germans and later the Belgians) ruled over the native Africans of the country, they found it expedient to use the Tutsi as intermediaries.

In the scientific community, also the difference in skin colors – black, brown or white – is nowadays not being taken seriously. It is being seen only as a matter of presence or absence of more or less quantities of dark pigments (dark or brown eumelanin) in a person's skin.

> „Eumelanin is produced through a multistage chemical process known as *melanogenesis*. […] In the human skin, melanogenesis is initiated by exposure to UV radiation causing the skin to darken. Eumelanin is an effective absorbent of light; the pigment is able to dissipate over 99.9 % of absorbed UV radiation. Because of this property, eumelanin is thought to protect skin cells from UVA and UVB radiation damage, reducing the risk of folate depletion and dermal degradation. […] Studies have shown a lower incidence for skin cancer in individuals with more concentrated melanin, i.e. darker skin tone."[2] (italics by S. Sarkar)

A layperson then asks: if all groups ("races") of humans of today were originally Africans, how did some of them become white? Palaeogeneticists explain this process as a result of the usual biological evolution through spontaneous mutations and natural selection. Thus, until about 7 to 8 thousand years ago, the skin color of European hunter-gatherer Homo Sapiens was dark like that of their African ancestors. Some of the first farmers who migrated from the Fertile Crescent of the Middle East (Syria, Iraq, Southern Turkey, the Nile Valley of Egypt and Israel) to Europe, carried in their genome the two genes responsible for pale skin color.

Now, sunshine is necessary for a chemical process essential for the health of human beings, namely production of vitamin D in the body itself. In European climatic conditions – with long dark winters and short, often clouded summers – the two genes responsible for pale skin proved to be of great evolutionary advantage: pale skin, namely, „provides better absorption qualities of ultraviolet radiation, which helps the body to synthesize higher amounts of vitamin D for bodily processes such as calcium development."[3] That was the reason why progenies of those immigrants from the Fertile Crescent who had carried the two said pale-skin genes in their genome rapidly proliferated in Europe.

Against the background of this knowledge, it sounds funny (to say the least) when a group of people in Western Europe and North America, namely the *White Supremacists*, put down the roughly two centuries old all-round domination of the world by these two regions to the white skin of the majority of the people living there.

Historians, who have tried to find the reasons for this domination have named other factors that played an important role in this development. In my youth, I had read that it was the Mediterranean climate and the warmth of the Gulf Stream that presented Southern and Western Europe the best conditions for prosperity and better living conditions. Ian Morris (2010) has stressed the role of geography: For example, the relative proximity of the huge American continent which enabled the Europeans to conquer and colonize it and then to exploit its vast resources. Jared Diamond (1998) has stressed inter alia inventions and spread of agriculture which led to population growth and growth of power. But all that is another subject.

Nobody can deny that in history, apart from the killings in regular wars between kingdoms and empires, states and nations, there has been brutal treatment of the defeated or subdued "others" (be they called a race, an ethnie, or, as in India, a caste). There has been, for example, enslaving, torturing, and lynching of the Blacks in Southern USA, Holocaust of the Jews in Nazi Germany, or crass discriminatory segregation of the Blacks from the whites in the South African Republic, the formers' own country. And nobody can deny that the white perpetrators of these barbarities thought of themselves as a race, believing in the ideology that there are superior and inferior *races* of humans. Such discriminatory treatment of "the others" cannot therefore be called anything other than *racism*.

This presentation of the topic race/racism can be best concluded with a quote from Max Weber (1997: 15):

„A [particularly] problematic source of social action […] is 'race identity': common inherited and inheritable traits that actually derive from common descent. Of course, *race creates a 'group' only when it is subjectively perceived as a common trait*: this happens only when the neighborhood or the mere proximity of racially different persons is the basis of joint (mostly political) action, or conversely, when some common experiences of the members of the same race are linked to some antagonism against members of an *obviously* different group." (italics by S. Sarkar)

The Others

Today, such barbaric brutalities as cited above do not generally happen anymore, not, at least, on a large scale and not on the grounds of a belief in the existence of and belonging to a superior race. What, however, still exists are milder or less brutal, and subtler forms of oppression or discrimination against the "others" (e.g., looking down upon, sneering at).

For example, when a white house owner in Europe or North America refuses to let a room to a black student from Africa, even though he can pay the rent, or when a black African discriminates in some or other way against another black African, which often happens in the African continent. E.g., a few years ago, there were violent riots in the South African Republic – between immigrants from the neighboring African countries and the locals, the citizens of the South African Republic, the only industrialized country in southern Africa. The locals attacked the immigrants and ransacked their shops and huts complaining that the latter were taking away jobs and business opportunities from the locals. In this case, the target of the riots was not any particular ethnic group, as in Rwanda, because the immigrants came from many different neighboring countries and belonged to many different, unrecognizable ethnic groups.

We must acknowledge that groups of victims of discrimination become *the "others"* for various reasons. Their common characteristic is that they are *subjectively perceived* by the victimizer group as a threat of some kind. How should one dub such cases of discrimination? At the latest now we must get some clarity on concepts.

A scholar on the subject, George Frederickson (2002: 157). defined „the essence of racism as the ideas, practices, and institutions associated with a rigid form of ethnic hierarchy". He avoided the terms *race* or *racial hierarchy*, used instead *ethnie* and *ethnic*, but did not here coin the term *ethnicism* (or feeling of *ethnic superiority*). In this definition the whites (who believe in white supremacy or for some reason feel proud of being a white person) are understood to be an ethnie (ethnic group).

Another scholar, Anthony D. Smith, (1997: 27) has tried to remove the confusion. He writes:

> „*Ethnie* (ethnic communities) may [...] be defined as named human populations with shared ancestry myths, histories and cultures, having an association with a specific territory and a sense of solidarity." (italics by S. Sarkar)

Smith also writes: „[...] such communities have been widespread in all eras of history, at least since the onset of the Bronze Age in the Middle East and Aegian, when written records appear to recount communal exploits and chronicle ethnic vicissitudes [...]." Smith writes further:

> „[...] they still characterize many areas of the globe and are to be found even in the most modernized states of the industrialized world. I am not claiming that they have constituted the main mode of socio-cultural organization, let alone the sole one, even in pre-modern eras; only that they have been at least as important as other

forms of organization and culture, and that we therefore neglect them at our peril."

We know from recent history (cf. Diamond 2006) that in Rwanda, where both the Hutu and the Tutsi are black and African, the Tutsi lorded it over the Hutu. Some years ago, I saw in a broadcast of some TV-station a documentary report on a similar political conflict between the Hutu and the Tutsi in Burundi. The reporter approached a small group of Tutsi young men, who were sitting under a tree and gossiping. When the reporter asked them, what the problem between them and the Hutu was, the young people could not (or simply did not) at first say anything in reply. But then one of them opened his mouth and said in a disdainful tone and with a corresponding grimace (I still remember the sentence): „Ach, the Hutu, they are, they are just too stupid." Of course, a power struggle was going on there too, as in Rwanda, but this sentence expressed a feeling of ethnic superiority that had no basis.

So, today, when in everyday life, we hear a charge of racism, it may in reality be a case of discrimination, on whatever grounds, of one or more social groups by another that has the power to discriminate. In certain circumstances, it may even be a *general* xenophobia, to be worried about the effects of presence of too many foreigners in one's native country (too many non-whites in Europe).

Xenophobia

Human-ethologist Eibl-Eibesfeldt (1984: 129) writes about our "ambivalent" reaction to previously unknown persons (strangers/foreigners):

„In all cultures, one looks upon them with a certain reservation. […] Already a nursling is scared of a fellow human, even though it has never experienced anything bad from him. Certain signals of fellow humans frighten us, and that all the more, the more their exterior appears foreign to us. That does not mean that he only activates rejection/disapproval. We can also observe clear reactions of affection/liking. And the reservation can be overcome by coming to know the strangers. But at first, the stranger evokes reservation and suspicion, and that also among infants."

So, xenophobia can be regarded as having its roots in this innate reservation.

Let us now take some examples: In 1990, just before and/or after the reunification of Germany (when the border gates between the two states had been opened) many Polish small farmers and traders travelled from villages bordering Germany to Berlin, which had become bigger through reunification, to sell their fresh food products. At the end of the day, before returning home, they bought with their sales proceeds many cheap industrial consumer goods in German supermarkets and sold them in Poland, thus making hefty profits. But the numerous "Polish markets" that, in this way, sprouted in Berlin were not welcome to all Berliners. The Poles were often attacked by those who hated their presence in Berlin for some or other reason. It was guessed that the local German small traders saw in the Polish markets foreign competitors. They simply hated foreign competitors, even Poles, who were white, Christian, and Europeans. Another suspect group were the German Neo-Nazis, who were on the rise after the fall of the socialist system in the GDR.

In those days, understandably, the colored people, the blacks and the browns had more to fear in East Germany than the white Polish marketers. There had even been some cases of black people dying as a result of severe injuries suffered in some violent attack. Colored people were therefore generally afraid of travelling to East Germany.

As the above examples show, I believe, the hatred was against *foreigners* rather than against any particular "race". This understanding of mine has been corroborated by later events and observations. Thus, in August 1992, in *Rostock-Lichtenhagen* (ex GDR), there was a 3 – 4 days long siege of a big house, in which mostly redundant immigrant workers from Vietnam were living. The attackers, a mob of some 3000 local Germans, started with pelting stones and bottles at these foreigners. But finally, the house was set on fire to the applause of many in the mob. The police did not take any action to prevent the outrageous attacks. On the contrary, at a certain point during the mob action, they even withdrew from the front[4].

Being a South Asian, I could not but take notice of the existence of "racism" in the UK. It was in the 1980s that I read and heard about the racist and radical rightist British

National Party (BNP) and of so-called *"Paki-bashing"*. "Paki" referred to all South Asians, not only to those from Pakistan, but also from India, Bangladesh and Sri Lanka. And "bashing" very often really meant violent assault. But it also meant casting slurs on Pakistanis/South Asians. Apart from common geography and their South Asian origin, there is only one common feature among people from these countries: they are on average brown colored. If it were for their skin color that they were hated, then, of course, one could call this phenomenon racism. But then the large number of people from the Caribbeans should have been the preferred victims of the racists, which was not the case. I learnt later that the people from Pakistan and Bangladesh understood Paki-bashing as an expression of Islamophobia.

But before and after the *Brexit* process (2016 – 2019), i.e. exit of the UK from the EU (European Union), it was the "large" number of Poles and other East Europeans who were the preferred targets of hatred and often violent attacks. But why these people? Weren't they all white, European, and Christian?

The *main* reason for all these phenomena has not been "race", i.e. physiognomy (e.g., skin color or shape of the nose), nor a general antipathy toward foreigners (the others). It has been the economic condition of the masses. Before 2016, because the UK had become a member of the EU, citizens of all EU countries could freely immigrate into the UK and search for (better paid) jobs and opportunities for small businesses, such as groceries and repair shops. Large numbers of workers, skilled and unskilled, and unemployed people from the relatively underdeveloped Eastern European EU member countries, particularly from Poland, took advantage of this rule and "flooded" the UK job market and rented into the scarce "affordable", i.e. relatively cheap, housings. The "Polish plumber" became the notorious symbol for this phenomenon, not only in the UK, but also in France.

The British underclass, but also workers in the low-wage sectors perceived this development as a threat to their vital economic interests. They protested and revolted in various forms, one of which was occasionally some or other kind of slur and violent actions against the East European immigrants. Brexit was largely the result of such resentments. The aforementioned phenomenon of "Paki-bashing" was also, at least partly if not largely, a consequence of preceding similar large-scale immigration of South Asian working people from Commonwealth countries and East Africa. The case of poor black immigrants in the South African Republic, who were violently maltreated by poor black citizens of the country, is also a corroboration of this view.

I can also submit here some evidence of another kind in support of this view. When, as mentioned above, redundant Vietnamese immigrant workers in Eastern Germany were being despised and also occasionally attacked, the Japanese, who were mostly resident businessmen, executives of Japanese companies, or tourists, were at risk of being mistaken for Vietnamese and also bashed up. To avoid this possibility, they were advised by the Japanese embassy never to go out without wearing a full suit, and to paste a label on the windshield of their car stating that it was Japanese owned (or some such words). I think, in this and similar cases, not only did the personal status – here a redundant foreign worker, and there a foreign business executive – make a difference. It also made a difference that the Vietnamese came from a poor underdeveloped country and the Japanese from a rich industrialized G-7 country.

Another example of a similar attitude is the system of offering a "Golden Passport". Several relatively poor EU countries offer moneyed foreign nationals immediate citizenship if they invest a stipulated few million Dollars in their economy, while they turn away the compatriots of these new citizens if they stand at the border as asylum seekers.

Of course, there are several visible and invisible factors of varying importance that are involved in the treatment a foreigner receives in the host country. Yet I feel tempted to formulate a general rule: If one is a foreigner and his country of origin is known, then, generally, the treatment he would be meted out would be proportional to the per capita GDP of his native country. This can be corroborated by observing the difference in the treatment received by e.g. a Yemeni or Syrian Arab and that received by an Arab e.g. from Saudi Arabia or UAE or Qatar.

Immigrants – Welcome and Unwelcome, Refugees – Genuine and False

According to the Global Trend Report of the UNHCR, globally, at the end of 2022, there were 108.4 million people who were fleeing their home. Included in this figure were both internally displaced persons (IDPs), i.e., those who sought refuge in a different part of their native country, and those who sought asylum in a foreign country. The latter groups of people often constitute a problem for relations between peoples, particularly in many prosperous industrialized countries, where they are not unequivocally welcome. Their presence there often contains conflict potential of various kinds.

Apart from those who flee their home due to some or other act of nature beyond control – flood, drought, earthquake etc. – or for being a victim of political oppression, man-made catastrophes such as war, civil war or large-scale violent disorder, there are those who are in reality immigrants (also called "economic refugees"). They are not victims of any of the things mentioned just above. They are only *seeking a better life* in some other country where the pastures are greener than in their native country. They are generally unemployed or unemployable young persons, or persons with a low income. And, in their native country, they generally do not have a perspective nor any hope of a better life in the near future. They enter, legally or illegally, a prosperous and/or industrialized country, sometimes gate-crashing into it.

We have seen innumerable documentary news-films of such attempts – some of them really dangerous. We have seen e.g. African daredevils trying to climb over 6 meters high barbed wire fences around the Spanish exclaves in Morocco, Ceuta and Melilla, and the Police there trying to prevent their landing. We have seen attempts to cross the Mediterranean Sea in overloaded dinghy boats, the foot marches of thousands of Central Americans to the United States via Mexico, and many other such things.

Now, if it is true, as I am convinced it is, that there are limits to growth, and hence limits to growth of standard of living of all in all countries, then it is understandable that hundreds of thousands of South and Central Americans, Africans, Asians, and, in general, *most people* in the Global South have lost hope of a better future in their own country. But this disappearance of hope is also taking place in the Global North, slowly, of course, but surely. The bon mot "No future" was after all coined in the Global North.

Humanism, expressed in such slogans as "Only one race: the human race", has all along been only an ideal written down in beautiful texts or proclaimed in beautiful speeches. I have heard one such speech by a young woman, who is engaged in NGO work for saving migrants trying to cross the Mediterranean Sea. She said inter alia: „All humans have the right to live where they want to." She gave this speech at a big rally organized jointly by Fridays for Future and the German Federation of Trade Unions.

And I read part of a text published in 2015 as a position paper (Migration Charter) by a group of theologians of Switzerland[5]:

„In a migration policy that is based on the principles of equality, justice, and solidarity, the basic right to choose one's home freely stands at the center. Universally valid right to choose one's home freely is the condition for ensuring that migration can take place also for small and endangered people in dignity. Migration must not be criminalized and disparaged any more." (translated by S. Sarkar)

But have the authors of such texts ever asked themselves why such ideals couldn't ever become reality for the vast majority of human beings? Already one of the authors of the Bible knew „The spirit is willing, but the flesh is weak." Or one could say like Faust said in another context (in Goethe's Faust I) „Zwei Seelen wohnen, ach, in meiner Brust" (two souls, alas, live in my breast).

To continue with our theme in this section, in 2015 - 2016, when about one million refugees from the Global South, mostly from war-torn Syria, threatened to gate-crash into Germany, most Germans were worried. But spurred on by some idealist activists and journalists, hundreds of Germans also came to the railway stations, where the first Trains with the refugees arrived, and welcomed them with sweets, toys and other gifts.

In this case, not an individual was feeling torn, but a whole people, the Germans, later the Europeans. In those days and in subsequent months and years, I remember, there were many German politicians and other public figures who criticized Angela Merkel, the then Federal Chancellor of Germany, for her solitary late-night decision in favor of an open-arm reception of so many refugees. She retorted, in the general sense: „If I have to beg to be excused for giving shelter to victims of war and oppression with a friendly face, then this is not my country."

But the human species is not a creation of any God, it was created in the process of evolution, the operating principles of which have been sufficiently uncovered by scientists. Today, we have no problem in accepting

(1) that like most animals, most humans too try to survive individually, fight against enemies or run away, if the enemy is too strong or if the danger is too overwhelming. And when means of sustenance are scarce, e.g. during a famine, we observe survival of the fittest.

(2) And, like animals, individual humans as well as groups of humans try to defend their current territory and/or to occupy new territory.

If we bear these two behavior patterns of humans in mind, then it becomes easier to understand the flow of refugees and migrants into Europe and the USA – generally speaking, into the rich Global North – as well as the hostile reactions of probably the majority of the present-day, established citizens of the favorite target countries of the Global North (which also includes Australia, New Zealand and Japan).

The flow of refugees and migrants into Europe and the USA had started long ago. Originally, they were of great advantage to the economy and the established citizens of the host countries. They had their cheap unskilled laborers and their cheap domestics. Immigrants from periphery countries were not only gladly tolerated in the highly industrialized ones. In many cases, they were also recruited in their native countries. For instance, during the postwar boom period, German industries actively recruited laborers in the Eastern parts of Turkey (Anatolia) on a large scale. But the boom ended around the middle of the 1970s. When the economy started stagnating or showing a negative trend, the German Federal government wanted the Turkish "guest workers" to go back home. But the Germans soon realized that they had miscalculated when they recruited these "guest workers". As a German publicist wrote in those days (in the general sense): we wanted to import labor power, but what came were human beings. The Turkish "guest" workers wanted to live in Germany with their families. They wanted to "enjoy" the German social welfare benefits they had a right to. In 1982, I saw graffiti on walls: "Turks, go away from Germany." And I heard comments, directed at picnicking Turkish families, such as „Oh, they have converted the park into Anatolia."

In the European Union, there were two categories of "guest workers".

(1) Many came from the less developed EU countries to the rich and highly industrialized ones. Germany attracted many workers from Southern Italy, Portugal, Spain, Greece and the then Yugoslavia. Such people were white, Christian and European, and have had some education. They were easily integrated into German society, or they went back home when their native countries also developed industries and offered satisfactory employment opportunities.

(2) But the Turks, Kurds, Arabs and about half of the African immigrants came with a different religion and

culture, Islam and Islamic. They stayed on in the EU, partly because their native countries could not achieve enough economic development to keep pace with their population growth, let alone to reabsorb the emigrated workers and their children, if they returned.

They also stayed on because life in the EU has generally been much better and freer. In the course of time, they also became citizens of EU countries, but they, most of them, refused to, or could not, get integrated into the European societies in the midst of which they were living. They also did not miss anything; their number was large enough and growing fast enough to have a society of their own within the larger society of their host country – complete with their food shops, cultural institutions, mosques etc. Among the native population, however, this generated a lot of animosity or ill feeling toward them. For instance, it was thought that such immigrants took advantage of the generous social benefit rules of the rich EU countries, but did not contribute enough to the prosperity of their host countries. In the heydays of Islamic terrorism, they were also suspected of harboring terrorists among them, and supporting terrorist activities and other reactionary Rightists.

Against this background, there appeared in 2010, in Germany, a very provocative and controversial book that gave scholarly expression to the suspicions and ill feelings just mentioned above: Thilo Sarrazin's bestseller *Deutschland Schafft Sich Ab – Wie Wir Unser Land aufs Spiel Setzen* (Germany Eliminates Itself – How We are Jeopardizing Our Country). The author reproached German political leaders and government employees for being naive toward the consequences of uncontrolled immigration. According to him, due to the low birth rate of present-day Germans, the population is diminishing and becoming less intelligent, while the social burdens are growing with growing immigration. This problem was not even being mentioned due to "political correctness".

He came down particularly hard on Muslim immigrants, who, according to him, have a higher birth rate and are overrepresented among recipients of social benefit payments. He reproached them for building a *parallel society* in their host countries and for not encouraging educational ambition among their children. He even raised the specter of *"conquest through birth rate"*. He recommended that EU societies should make it clear to the immigrants that they

> „should learn the language, earn their livelihood through work, have educational ambition for their children, adapt themselves to the mores and customs of Germany, and they should become German in the course of time. […] But we do not want to have any national minorities. Those who want to remain a Turk or Arab and desire this also for their children, they had better stay in their country of origin. And those who are mainly interested in the blessings of the German social welfare system, they are not welcome at all."[6]

Five years later, in France, Michel Houellebecq's novel *Submission* was published – exactly on the day (7.1.2015) the Islamist attack on the Paris office of *Charlie Hebdo* happened, in which 12 persons were killed. It is a fiction, no doubt, but the story has much relevance to the present-day reality. In the fiction, a situation is depicted, in which France was convulsed by violent race riots between radical rightists and radical Islamists. Everywhere houses, cars, shops were burning, people were being killed. That was also election time. In order to prevent radical rightist candidate Marine Le Pen's victory in the presidential election, Socialists and Conservatives entered an alliance with the moderate Islamists. The charismatic Muslim leader Ben Abbes was thus elected as President. It was 2022. Islamization of France began.

Up to here, it is fiction, published in 2015. What is not fiction, however, is that, in the last days of June 2023, Paris was indeed burning, exactly speaking, its suburb *Nanterre*, and many other towns and cities such as Marseilles, where there are *banlieues*, that are mostly populated by Black African, and Nord African Muslim Arab immigrants. Paris had burnt before, in 2005, when two young men from a banlieue, who were being chased by some policemen, died of electrocution.

Fact is also that the French and, generally speaking, the Europeans are ill at ease with the continuous and growing flow of refugees and illegal immigrants from the African and Middle East countries, the majority of whom are Muslims. Some years ago, a Dutch rightist politician said: „I am afraid, we are losing our country." And I heard a German rightist politician say in TV: „If we do not grant asylum to an Afghan, he can go back to his country. But if I lose my country, I have nowhere to go." On other occasions I have heard of the fear of a population substitution ("Bevölkerungsaustausch").

Up to here, I have reviewed the macroeconomic and macro-political conditions in Europe that are generating conflict between groups of people. But immigration is (can be) a factor of conflict also at the ground (microeconomic) level. Here are two examples from Germany:

In bad times, an enterprise may have to retrench some workers of a particular plant. According to the prevailing rules for such cases, those in the workforce who are juniors or younger or have no family yet should go first. The seniors are spared, because they may find it hard to find a new job. Once it so happened that a senior German worker who had not married yet was retrenched, because his junior and younger Turkish colleague had not only married but also had two children. The German colleague expressed his anger publicly in front of a TV-camera, in words roughly like this: these people marry so early and produce children; so they are privileged.

The other example relates to the antipathy generated by the headscarf worn by many Muslim women. Once, one such woman who had got a job in a German company, was asked by the manager to work at the reception desk. She was also asked not to wear her headscarf while working at that position, because, the manager argued, that might put off would-be customers. The woman construed the order as religious discrimination. She went to court over the issue and won her case, much to the chagrin of her German colleagues.

Such ground-level matters are, however, *not wholly* determined by macroeconomic or macro-political factors. Also important are the cultural factors, for example, the degree of cultural tolerance prevailing among the population groups of a country, or how strongly members of population groups of a country feel about their identity – national, cultural and religious, or how resolutely they want to defend it.

All things considered, in all these conflict-laden matters, there is in each kind of cases a *socio-critical limit,* beyond which a simmering problem becomes explosive. In the case of radioactive Uranium-235 e.g., physicists can say exactly how much mass of this substance must be brought together before it becomes critical and then explodes. But nobody can quantify the *socio-critical limit* of anything which must not be exceeded in order to avoid a social explosion. That is not only a matter of numbers and proportions, but also of behavior, feeling, inurement, experience, etc.

Notes and References (Chapter 3)

1. https://en.wikipedia.org/wiki/Ethnicity (accessed: 18.4.2024): „An ethnicity or ethnic group is a group of people who identify with each other on the basis of perceived shared attributes that distinguish them from other groups. Those attributes can include a common nation of origin, or common sets of ancestry, traditions, language, history, society, religion, or social treatment. The term ethnicity is often used interchangeably with the term nation, particularly in cases of ethnic nationalism.

Ethnicity may be construed as an inherited or as a societally imposed construct. Ethnic membership tends to be defined by a shared cultural heritage, ancestry, origin myth, history, homeland, language, dialect, religion, mythology, folklore, ritual, cuisine, dressing style, art, or physical appearance. Ethnic groups may share a narrow or broad spectrum of genetic ancestry, depending on group identification, with many groups having mixed genetic ancestry."

2. https://en.wikipedia.org/wiki/Melanin (accessed: 19.4.2024), italics by S. Sarkar.

3. https://en.wikipedia.org/wiki/Light_skin (accessed: 19.4.2024)

4. https://www.dw.com/en/germany-remembers-the-rostock-anti-immigrant-riot-of-1992/a-62890639 (accessed: 20.4.2024)

5. https://www.migrationscharta.ch/manifest/ (accessed: 21.4.2024). The Migration Charter was published in fall 2015 by a loose group of Protestant-Reformed and Roman Catholic theologians from German-speaking Switzerland as a basic text for a new migration policy from a biblical-theological perspective.

6. https://de.wikipedia.org/wiki/Deutschland_schafft_sich_ab (accessed: 22.4.2024). Quoted from the 2nd edition of Sarrazin (2010), p. 326, translated by S. Sarkar.

Chapter 4

A Jungle of Collective Identities

Identity

In relation to other animals, i.e., as a species, we are all humans, one human race, Homo sapiens, one collective identity group. If we see a hungry tiger attacking a human, we rush to the latter's help, and try to shoo away the tiger. We are all Africans. (I have referred to this scientific wisdom in the foregoing chapter 3.) But that is only in theory so. In worldly matters, we do not behave as one human species. The exposition on the Hutu-Tutsi conflict (Ch. 2) as well as that on the illegal immigration and refugees problem in the foregoing chapter show that we humans are divided up in many groups and subgroups, each with a different *bundle* of identities pursuing conflicting interests.

So, we now also have to deal with the issue of identity in the already problems-ridden present-day world – identity of an individual, a community, a people, or a nation, ethnic identity, cultural identity, class identity etc. etc. It leads us to the questions: Who am I? Who is he? Who are we?[1] And in a huge nation state like India, we can ask ourselves: Are we all one people, just Indians? Or are we Assamese, Bengalis, Biharis, Tamils, Maharastrians etc. etc.? After all, each people has its own language!

When abroad, if asked, „Where are you from?", we have no problem stating „I am Indian". But in India, one expects a *differentiated* reply. We have to state our subnational, i.e., provincial or ethnic or language identity. An Indian from Patna, whose mother-tongue is Hindi, would not simply say he is North Indian. He would say he is Bihari. And a person from Uttarakhand, whose mother tongue is also Hindi, would say he is Garhwali.

In some cases, in problem situations, particularly under adverse economic circumstances, such *differentiation* can become conflict factors. But sometimes, also circumstances other than economic – e.g., foreign domination, crowding, party-political rivalries etc. – can play a causative role in conflict, alone or, as in most cases, mixed with economic grievances. In any case, the differences are there, they are real. In the past, since independence in 1947, India has experienced quite a few territorial border disputes among Indian peoples speaking different Indian languages. The differences have to be acknowledged, because they cannot be made to vanish.

The concept *identity* may relate to an individual, a more or less small group, or to a large, even very large group. That is why it is usual to speak of collective identity of a group, of a community. After all, no individual human lives alone. The members of a group, small or large, share some common feature(s) and/or interest(s) that make it clear to themselves as well as to others that they are an identity group.

The shared feature(s) can relate to the bodies of the people: skin color, shape of the nose and eyes, type of hair etc. That may lead to (self)identification as Blacks, White Caucasians with a long nose, Yellow Mongolians with a short nose etc. Scientists call this process of differentiation *pseudo speciation or quasi speciation*.[2] Among humans, they also can, and mostly do, relate to language, religion, world view (e.g., theist or atheist), political views, culture etc. To "culture" in the social-anthropological sense belong customs and traditions, traditional laws, mythology, traditional arts such as music, dance, drama, paintings, sculptures etc., even such material things as traditional clothing, housing, food/cooking etc. Such things taken together are called a person's or a group's cultural identity.

We have seen that in the case of the people of Rwanda, this process led in some hoary past to a division into two groups: *Hutu* and *Tutsi*. We have seen that despite some visibly different physical features, they are no longer called races, but ethnies or ethnic groups.[3] The main difference between them has not been their slightly different physical features, but their profession: The Hutu have been mainly small farmers and the Tutsi mainly herders. Here, the profession functioned as the main constituting factor of their collective identity.

Many other things *can* function, jointly and/or severally, as constituting factors of collective identity. It is also described (not defined) in cultural terms, and culture is a pretty loose thing. For example, in 1996, when a professor of Harvard University „asked his students whether anybody in the class could tell what his cultural identity was, one of them replied in a doubtless and self-evident tone: 'Of course, I am a New Yorker: I eat bagels, I read the Times and I walk fast. '" (Emcke 2010: 11). That is an ordinary man's way of describing his "cultural identity". In

India, a similar example would be if a Western Indian describes a Bengali's cultural identity in words like: „He is a Bengali; Bengalis like to eat rice and hot fish curry." But ask Bengali educated middle class persons about their cultural identity, and they might reply giving a short lecture on the subject (they love to talk a lot), stressing their mother tongue Bengali, the highly developed literature that they read, and *Rabindra sangeet* (songs written and composed by Rabindranath Tagore) that they sing. They might also refer to the history of Bengal, gloating over the fact that contact between Indian and European cultures began in Calcutta (Kolkata), West Bengal. Indeed, history and language appear to be two of the most important factors of identity building of a large group, whether we call it a nation, a tribe or an ethnie (ethnic group, ethnicity)[3].

To take two more examples from India, in case of the *Rajputs* in Rajasthan, their mother tongue (if we ignore the many dialects) is Hindi, the same as in the western part of Northern India. What constitutes their collective identity the most is their glorious and glorified military-historical tradition. In the case of the Sikhs, it is more their religion and appearance (the beard and the turban) than anything else. But martial tradition also plays a part in their identity. These things are somewhat arbitrary.

How arbitrary and how fast a process of identity building can be was demonstrated in a social-psychological experiment made in the USA in the 1950s:

22 randomly selected, well-behaved, eleven years old boys – all from white protestant middle class families – were invited to a summer camp in a beautiful natural

resort area. They were divided up into two groups, friends were separated. For some time, each group planned their adventure activities on their own and carried them through without supervision. Then the social-psychologists organized some sports competitions between the two groups, like for example, football matches, in which trophies could be won. At first everything took place in a fair and friendly atmosphere. But soon it became ugly. There were scuffles between the two groups, and insidious activities of each group against the other. The experimenters could observe the development of an us-versus-them mentality before they ended the experiment. (Wranham and Peterson 2001: 242f.)

Another example could be given from India, where a whole people – the Meitis of Manipur (in the Far East of India) – decided to give themselves an additional identity, namely that of a tribal people. I shall go into that story below.

Drawing on many more similar experiments as with the 11 years old US-American boys, also among grown-ups, the authors Wrangham and Peterson (2001: 244) come to the conclusion:

„Humans build groups very quickly, prefer their own group-members to outsiders, and do not take long to become aggressive to others. In principle, we hate such partialities. They lead to all kinds of isms – racism, sexism, ethnocentrism etc. Yet, with alarming levity, we fall victim to them again and again."

Let us take some, only some, examples of conflict arising from identity consciousness:

1. Tribal Conflicts in South Africa

Even when they have a common purpose, and a common enemy to fight against, it may also happen that two identity groups (tribes or ethnicities[3]) may have some disputes they cannot resolve amongst themselves. Thus, when the Dutch came to South Africa and started their settlers' colonies, the two largest tribes of this region, the Xhosa and the Zulu, of course, fought against the Dutch, but they could not agree on how to fight against the colonists. The Zulu fought violently and fiercely, but not the Xhosa. The latter tried the path of compromise by embracing change. Both failed in their endeavor. They accused each other of obstructing the resistance struggle.

After the end of Apartheid, not only the Xhosa and the Zulu, but all the tribes fought for power on tribal lines, not on political lines, of which they probably did not have any at all. Much Black blood was spilled in the struggle of the tribes for supremacy. But not their white oppressors' blood[4].

During the phase of establishing a constitution for South Africa and prior to the first free elections, bloodshed frequently occurred between *Inkatha*, a party of the Zulu, and the ANC cadre in Zulu areas. Inkatha leader Buthelezi also collaborated with the white forces.

2. The Chinese in Indonesia

The most extreme example of the identity question becoming a conflict factor is also one of the earliest. It comes from Indonesia, which became an independent nation state in 1949. Present-day statistical estimates of its total population range between 273 and 280 million comprising roughly 1300 ethnic groups who speak over 700 living languages. The official and national language of the country is *Bahasa Indonesia*, a standardized variety of *Malay*, that has been used for centuries as a *lingua franca*.

In such a variegated country, the Chinese, who represent only 1.2 percent of the population, have since long been considered to be an alien element, not belonging to the Indonesian people. Most of them had immigrated during the Dutch colonial rule, and they live mostly on the country's main island Java. After 1949, many felt compelled to leave the country. Non-citizen Chinese were no longer allowed to live in small towns, and so many lost their livelihood. The purpose of this move was to bring trade in rural regions under the control of Indonesian nationals.

In 1965 – 1966, in connection with the great massacre of communists of the country, the Chinese were also suspected of being communists. General Suharto, who had captured power, discovered a *"Chinese problem"*, which cried for solution. He started interfering in the matter of religion, faith and culture of the Chinese. Chinese language schools and cultural associations were closed down. Selling Chinese language books and use of Chinese ideographs were prohibited. The only Chinese language newspaper that was allowed was made to work under government control. Chinese names were Indonasianized. Public celebration of the Chinese New Year was prohibited. All these measures were later found to have gone too far. The intention to relax them was announced. But how much relaxation has taken place is unknown outside the country.

3. Turks in Germany

For a long time after the large-scale recruitment of unskilled and semi-skilled workers from peripheral European countries, Turkey and other non-European countries had begun in Germany, and even after their number had swelled to more than a million or two, conservative German politicians insisted that Germany was not an immigration country. In the early 1980s, I remember, when a recession had begun and the number of unemployed workers in West Germany had grown to over 2 million, the then Chancellor Helmut Kohl wanted the unemployed workers from Turkey and other non-European countries to go back to their native country. He offered to pay them the money back that they had contributed to the social insurance funds. That roughly was also the time, when I saw several radical rightist demonstrations against such foreigners and heard slogans such as "Germany for Germans, foreigners get out" ("Deutschland für Deutsche, Ausländer raus.") And I saw Graffiti like "Turks, get out of Germany".

But the Turkish and other foreign workers rejected Chancellor Kohl's offer. They had immigrated and wanted to make Germany their home. However, though they wanted to continue to live in Germany, the vast majority of them did not want to integrate themselves in German society. At heart, they remained Turks, Moroccans, and Arabs. Politically, their loyalty belonged to their country of birth. And culturally, their culture remained that of their childhood and youth or, if born in Germany, that of their parents' family.

In order to encourage and facilitate such people's integration[5] in German society and loyalty to the German state, the government greatly relaxed the citizenship law, retaining only one strong condition, namely the applicant must be ready to give up his original citizenship.

The vast majority of the immigrants gladly accepted the offer because of the many advantages of having a German passport, but some, particularly those from Turkey, did not want to give up their original, i.e., Turkish nationality. After getting their German citizenship, they secretly again applied for a Turkish passport, which they easily got.

When this misuse of the citizenship-offer came to light, the German public became angry and the government threatened to annul the newly acquired German citizenship of the offending persons. But such new German passport-holders who wanted to insist on their Turkish identity found a solution to the problem. They persuaded the Turkish government to issue them a card certifying that they were born in Turkey, or something similar to that.

It was apparently very important for them to insist and demonstrate that, although they had become citizens of

Germany, they had not become Germans and not ceased to be Turks. That is why every time Mr. Erdogan (President of Turkey) came to Germany, German Turks held in his honor a big rally, on which Mr. Erdogan spoke. I have seen TV-reports on such rallies. On one such occasion, a German reporter asked them why they had come to that rally, to which they replied by loudly shouting the slogan „Integration Yes, Assimilation No".

I once saw in a German TV program a short interview with an elderly average Turkish worker. The German moderator asked him whether he is German or Turk. The interviewee replied by assuring the moderator: „My president is Ms. Angela Merkel". When the moderator further asked him why he then had that card, which he had seen before, the interviewee replied: „That is for my identity."

Such a dichotomy in a human's personality can also lead to conflicts. Once, a high-ranking Turkish minister visited her compatriots in Holland and had wanted to speak at a rally. Members and supporters of her party (AKP) gave her a rousing reception at the railway station and wanted to immediately hold a rally on the street. The Dutch police however did not want to tolerate that and tried to forcibly clear the street. In the resulting scuffle, the police also used their batons. In the din, the TV man reported, some policeman shouted: „We must show them who the boss in this country is."

The Kurds

In Germany, I have had the opportunity to talk to several activists of the radical left. Among the people, parties and groups from Turkey are also some who are Kurdish. Most prominent among them are activists and sympathizers of the Workers' Party of Kurdistan (PKK), which is since long fighting for an independent, separate and socialist Kurdistan. I asked both groups, why at least the radical leftists from Turkey cannot work together? While the Turkish radical leftists said they would gladly do so, the Kurdish radical leftists said they cannot, because they are looked down upon in Turkey, are called derogatively Hill-Turks (Bergtürken). Moreover, there are also many Kurds in Syria and Iraq, with whom together they would like to build up their independent state Kurdistan. Their Kurdish identity does not allow them to feel at home in any of the two states.

As we know, the Kurds, exactly speaking, the followers of Abdulla Ocalan, who are organized in the PKK, are since long carrying on an armed struggle against the Turkish military. But the Kurds who live in the state of Iraq could be successfully pacified. They have arranged with the Iraqi authorities and live in their autonomous region in the North of Iraq.

4. Multiplicity of Ethnic Identities in India

We can also take an example from India, the multi-ethnic nation state per excellence. In the above-mentioned cases of Turks living in Germany and Holland, the separateness of their identity from that of the host people related to ethnicity and religion (all Turks living there presumably can speak German or Dutch respectively). In India, however, the main factor determining ethnic identity is language, generally speaking culture. Here we should speak of ethno-cultural (or ethno-linguistic) identity.

In an election period, the ruling party at the center, *Bharatiya* Janata Party (BJP, translated: Indian People's Party), sent a large number of Hindi-speaking campaign volunteers from their strongholds in Northern India (the Hindi Belt) to the eastern province of West Bengal, where Bangla is the language of the vast majority. *Trinamul National Congress* (TNC, transl.: Grassroots National Congress), the party that has been ruling in West Bengal, made the point that the BJP had no base in Bangla-speaking West Bengal, which is why they had to depend on *"Bahiragatos"* (transl.: people coming from outside) to do electioneering in West Bengal. This argument apparently worked; the BJP lost. But the fact that Indians from another province were labelled as "outsiders", speaks volumes about the quality of Indian nationhood.

An ugly blot in the concept of Indian nationhood is that the Hindu society, consisting of the vast majority of Indians, is divided and sub-divided in many castes and sub-castes, many of them having a rigidly fixed, very low social and (mostly also) economic status. There are also many tribal peoples whose place has always been outside and below the Hindu society. In the early years of independent India (the early 1950s), the ruling elite followed a policy of abolishing this caste system and lifting the lower castes (and the tribal peoples) to the mainstream. However, with this good intention, they did the wrong thing to achieve their goal. They introduced by law a whole system of educational, economic and job-related privileges and favors (e.g., reservations of jobs and seats in universities) for members of the lower castes and the tribes. But they achieved the opposite; they perpetuated the caste system instead. Since belonging to a lower caste or "scheduled" tribe became a gateway to better education, and economic and career success, nobody who "enjoyed" it wanted to lose this kind of "low" status.

What perversity and how much violent conflict this system can lead to was recently demonstrated in the small province/state of Manipur in the far North-East of India. In the beginning of May 2023, the media reported from this remote province that largescale violence, arson, mayhem and killings were taking place, in which the Meitei and Kuki, a tribal people, were pitted against each other. For those who live outside this state, the news came suddenly. The Meitei constitute the majority (53 %) of the population of the state, and the great majority of them are Hindu and agriculturists. They live on the plains of Imphal Valley, and – not being a scheduled tribe – are excluded from owning or buying a piece of protected forest lands. The Kuki are the largest of the scheduled tribes in Manipur and the major beneficiaries of the law that grants tribal people the privilege of being allowed not only to live in the protected forests but also to own or buy a piece of land there.

The proximate cause of the violent conflict was a ruling of the High Court of Manipur ordering the state government to recommend to the central government that the *Meitei* people of the state be included in the list of "scheduled tribes". But why did the Meitei at all demand to be recognized as a scheduled tribe, which they clearly were not? They belonged after all to the Hindu majority of India! People in the know say because they too desired the right to buy and own land in the protected forests. The Kuki and the other tribes saw in this ruling of the High Court the danger of losing all their privileges. For a privilege ceases to be one if all people enjoy it. They started demonstrating and protesting against this High Court ruling. But the animosity between these two ethnic groups were so deep-rooted and had so many facets that it did not remain at that level. I cannot here go into greater details.[6]

But one general and basic factor of conflict that I have mentioned earlier in this book, viz. population growth, should also be mentioned in this context. The estimated population of Manipur in 2023 is approximately 3.65 million. In the decade 2001 – 2011 it grew by 17.68 %. In the space of 110 years – from 1901 to 2011 – the population of Manipur grew tenfold.[7]

Malaysia is another such example. This, compared to India, relatively small nation state is inhabited by four peoples – the Malays (50.4 %), the Chinese (23.7 %), the Indians (7.1 %), and the indigenous peoples (generally, collectively called Dayaks) the rest.[8] There has been tension in the country between the Chinese, who dominated in industry and commerce, and the Malay majority, who felt they were coming off second best. At the instance of the majority, laws were passed requiring employers to give preference to "Bhumiputras" (sons of the soil).

5. Identity of Immigrants

The theme of migration reminds me of a saying: „Blood is thicker than water". There have been immigrants into Germany from Russia (formerly Soviet Union) who were not only welcome, but also got a right to immigrate, because they were regarded as Germans by blood ("Blutdeutsche") by virtue of their descent, i.e. one or more of their forefathers had emigrated to Russia. When, two to three centuries later, such Russian citizens of German blood (Russodeutsche) perceived better economic opportunities in the highly industrialized and more prosperous West Germany and wanted to migrate back to Germany, there was no problem. They were all welcome.

But when, in the early 1990s, the Vietnamese who had been "guest workers from a brotherly country" in the erstwhile GDR (German Democratic Republic), wanted to stay on in reunited Germany, they were not welcome at all. They were just tolerated, often reluctantly.[9] Similarly, when, in 2015 – 2016 and thereafter, Syrians, Iraqis, Afghans, Pakistanis, Sub-Saharan Africans etc. started coming, or rather gate-crashing, they were not welcome to all Germans.

Hardly anybody saw here an instance of racial discrimination. For the Germans in Germany, immigration of Russo-Germans was something like coming home of prodigal sons. For them, Russo-Germans were all Germans, they all belonged to the same people. But refugees from Asia who gate-crashed into Germany in 2015 - 2016 were foreigners. Starry-eyed idealists, however, thought otherwise. I once saw them holding high a placard that said: "No borders, No nations!". It does not sound merely like an anti-racist slogan; it is rather a declaration of belief in international humanism. It was in fact used to protest against radical rightist actions and positions against refugees from the Global South.

Let us remember that before and after the *Brexit* referendum, for a large percentage of British people, the Polish and other East European immigrants in the UK were not only not welcome, they were also, in some cases, violently attacked by the British pro-Brexit people. That in this case, almost all involved were Whites and Christians, and for many years citizens of the EU, did not help in generating the feeling "we are all Europeans".

These phenomena need to be understood. In the case of Germans welcoming Russo-Germans, we see a feeling of German identity based on common descent (similar to tribal identity) at work. In the case of the majority of the British people, i.e., those who supported Brexit, we see the absence of a feeling of European identity, although the UK was a member of the European Union and also geographically belongs to the continent of Europe.

6. Religion as collective identity

„We are Muslims, our religion is Islam", said the young Ayman al-Zawahiri [later to become the second top leader of Al Qaeda] in a very loud and defiant tone in a court room in Cairo, where he stood trial for a terrorist attack by his political friends. He did not say he and his co-accused friends were Egyptians, nor that they were Arabs. Sheikh

Mujibur Rahman, on the other hand, another Muslim, who led the independence struggle of his native country, the then East Pakistan and today's Bangladesh, did not bother about his being a Muslim. Instead, he related his collective identity to his being born in Bengal, about one-third of which belonged to India, and to his mother tongue being Bangla, which is also the mother tongue of the people living in the Western, i.e., the Indian part of Bengal. Urdu, the official language of the then Pakistan, whose citizen Mujibur Rahman had been until the success of the independence struggle in 1971, did not play any part in his feeling of identity.

To take another case, the young Muslim suicide bombers from Pakistani immigrant families living in the UK, who perpetrated their terrorist attack in 2005 in the London tube-rail system, were citizens of the UK. They were born and brought up and went to school in that country. For them, however, their collective identity was, like Al-Zawahiri's, being a Muslim. They felt angry, indeed oppressed, because, as they saw it, the British and the Americans were killing Muslims in Iraq and Afghanistan. They took revenge by killing British citizens and, incidentally, some citizens of other countries.

In India, it had been popular to maintain that, before independence, the British rulers followed a policy of divide and rule, that they created or at least stoked the Hindu-Muslim conflict in order to be able to continue their rule. This does not convince me. Although, generally speaking, most ordinary people of these two big religious communities of India may always have desired peaceful co-existence and followed the precept *live and let live*, although many of them even had friends and good neighbors in the other religious community, there have always been many fanatics, who saw in the other religious community opponents of their own vision of future India or obstacles to their personal ambitions.

The fanatics also had a theoretical basis for their stance. It was the Two-Nations-Theory. Mohammed Ali Jinnah, founder-father of Pakistan propounded it in the following words: „Hindustan [i.e., India] is neither one country, nor its inhabitants are one nation. This is a sub-continent which consists of many nations, of which the Hindus and Muslims are two major nations."[10].

Before him, other ideologues had stressed the unbridgeable gap between the religious beliefs and practices of Hindus and Muslims, their two cultures, their languages and their social systems. Expressed in modern-day terminology, "The Muslims apprehended that they would lose their identity if they remained a part of Hindu society". I have heard interviews with Pakistanis touching upon this question. Nobody blamed the British for the partition of India. The essence of what I have heard and read is as follows: If India had not been divided, then all Indian Muslims would now be living as a disadvantaged minority in a country dominated by the Hindu majority. This they refused to accept. I can understand this fear. After all, before the British conquered India, the Muslims had ruled over the greater part of India and enjoyed the privileges of a ruling minority. And some of their ruling kings and emperors had not treated the Hindu majority gently.

On the other hand, many Hindus could not forget that Muslim armies from faraway central Asia and Afghanistan invaded, plundered and finally conquered India at a time of weakness and decadence of its Hindu kings. They wanted to reestablish the putative glory of Hindu India. Not only the Indian Muslims – organized in the party *Muslim League* – propounded the *Two-Nations Theory*, but also radical Hindus – organized in the party *Hindu Mahasabha* [transl.: Great Congregation of Hindus] and their militant association *Rashtriya Swayam Sevak Sangh* (RSS) [State Volunteers Association] – asserted that Hindus and Muslims of India are two different antagonistic nations[11].

Those who have some knowledge of European history know about the *Thirty Years War* (1618 – 1648) between the Catholics and the Protestants, in which central Europe was devastated. That war was fought under the leadership of the respective monarchs of the two confessions. In India, both before and after 1947 – when the two independent states, India and Pakistan, were created – large-scale massacres and displacement of several million Indians took place. The Hindus were displaced from Pakistan and the Muslims from India. The former found refuge in India and the latter in Pakistan. The power of the till then all-powerful British empire had ceased to exist. The massacres and forcible displacements took place under the leadership of the fanatic gangsters of the two religions, who could successfully rouse the fury of the masses.

All progressives, leftists, and otherwise modern people always underestimate the power of traditional religious faiths. In Europe – generally speaking, in the presumably progressive Western cultures – the religions are no longer as powerful as before. But still, there, Islamophobia has raised its head again. The Prime Minister of Hungary, a member state of the EU, can proudly say that his country will not take in any Muslim refugees, but only some Christian ones.

There is no doubt that the indigenous white and Christian population of Europe has grounds to be wary. One can justify this Islamophobia as a reaction to the killing campaigns of Islamic terrorists all over the world, including in Europe. Both the actions and reactions demonstrate the power of religious identities as factors of conflict. The memory of Arab-Muslim conquest of Spain, the Crusades, and then the Reconquista of Spain cannot be erased from the mind of the respective peoples. History lessons in schools guarantee that. Meanwhile, Shias and Sunnis, the two major confessions of Islam are continuing their ca. 1400 years old bloody fight for supremacy in the Islamic world.

In India, where, after the partition of the country in 1947, we thought the conflict has been settled for ever, Hindu-Muslim conflicts still break out now and then. It requires only a small incident, that is interpreted as a provocation, to unleash attacks on the Muslim minority by Hindu reactionary forces.

Examples from history, including recent history, show that not only defending one's religious identity serves as motivation for aggressive and/or vengeful behavior. Some religions – Islam and Christianity, to mention only the most prominent ones –are laden with missionary zeal.

Such zeal is often mixed with the desire to expand the territory or influence of a kingdom and/or regime and with need to occupy new territory for an expanding population. In its beginning, Buddhism had a missionary zeal. But, being a non-violent religion, it apparently lost any aggressiveness that it might once have possessed, although we do not know for sure whether in the past, it played any role in the wars waged by Thai and Burmese kings.

Even a section of the Indian Sikhs – a small minority in the Indian subcontinent, – who too, in 1947 and thereafter, fled or were expelled from the newly founded Pakistan, wanted, since before 1947, to create a new independent state based on their religion and culture in the Indian province of Punjab, where they formed the majority of the population. It was to be called Khalistan, land of the Khalsa. It must also be mentioned here that in the case of this movement, also the language of the Sikhs, namely Punjabi, played an important role.

In the 1980s, they even started a militant rebellion against the Indian state , but it was soon suppressed by the Indian security forces. In retaliation, they bombed and destroyed two Indian passenger planes over the Atlantic and killed the then Prime Minister of India, Indira Gandhi. The Hindus retaliated in Delhi, the capital city of India, by killing about 2000 poor Sikhs.

7. Ethno-religious identity conflict in Northern Ireland

It must still be fresh in the memory of all Europeans how in North Ireland, Irish Catholics and Protestants of English and Scottish immigrant heritage fought a 30 years long bloody guerilla war – the former (called the *Nationalists*) for the liberation and integration of the territory in the Irish Republic and the latter (called the *Unionists*) for holding on to its status as a part of Great Britain.

Ireland, the whole island, had been a British colony up until 1921, when, after a long independence struggle, the Republic of Ireland was founded, but not before the island was partitioned into the Republic and the territory of North Ireland, the protestant majority of which refused to live under Catholic rule.

The cultural divide has another dimension: The Protestants of Northern Ireland are descendants of the much-hated settlers from colonialist Great Britain, i.e., outsiders. who occupied the land. Actually, as in most similar other cases, the settlers had been poor peasants and farmhands, who were compelled to leave their country. They however, for generations, still felt attached to their country of origin. The Nationalists are Catholics and descendants of the original population predating the conquest by the British. Moreover, under British colonial rule, they had been victims of many kinds of discrimination, which generated an angry reaction resulting in what is known as the "Troubles", i.e., the period of violent fights, in which more than 3600 people were killed, especially in the period between 1968 and 1994.

The violent conflict ended with the Good Friday Agreement of 1998 (10th April) and the following referendum (22nd May), which ascertained that the majority of the people of North Ireland wanted the territory to remain a part of the United Kingdom. It was also agreed that the constitutional status of the territory may be changed in future when and if all parties want to change it. North Ireland today enjoys a devolved government like Scotland and Wales.

Although Catholics in their majority demand integration in the Irish Republic, it is not as if in elections they all vote for the *Sin Féin* or the Social Democrats. Many prefer the conservative policies of the Unionist parties. Similarly, not all of them speak *Gaelic*, the original language of all Irish people. Today, grown-ups in 95 % of all households speak mainly English, though Gaelic is the second official language of the territory.

8. Ethno-Cultural Identity Conflict in Sri Lanka

A combination of three strong identities – ethnicity, religion and language – standing opposed to another combination of three same categories of identities in the same country; that can become explosive. And that indeed happened in Sri Lanka in the years between 1983 and 2009.

In this island state situated very close to India, the population of ca. 22 million consists of several ethnicities: The majority are the Sinhalese with 74.9 %. The Tamil form the second biggest ethnic group with 15.4 %. Another large ethnic group are the Sri Lankan Moors with 9.2 %.

The so-called "others", added together, come to a negligible 0.5 %[12].

The percentage figure for the Tamil is usually subdivided into *Sri Lankan Tamil* (11.2 %) and *Indian Tamil* (4.2 %). The existence of Sri Lankan Tamil on the island can be traced back to ancient times (2nd century BCE), when perhaps the present-day distinction between the two states, Sri Lanka and India, did not exist. The Indian Tamil (like the Protestant Scots in Northern Ireland) are clearly descendants of immigrants from South India, who were recruited in the 19th and early 20th century for working in the coffee, tea and rubber plantations.

The Tamil – ethnically Indians, Hindu by religion, and speaking Tamil, a South Indian Dravidian language – felt oppressed and discriminated against by the majority ethnic group, the Sinhalese – Buddhist by religion, and speaking Sinhala, an Indo-Aryan language. They rebelled, built up their own army (the *Tamil Tigers*), and fought a long civil war against the armed forces of the state in an effort to create a separate and independent state of their own in the North and North-East of the island.

The grievances of the Tamil minority did not only relate to discrimination at the level of everyday administration of law. They were also very much concerned about discriminatory policy decisions at the highest political level. Thus, in 1956, Prime Minister Bandaranaike declared himself to be the „defender of the besieged Sinhalese Culture"[13]. In his zeal in that role, he got the "Sinhala Only Act" passed, which recognized Sinhala as the only official language of the government. The Act was later partially reversed, and today, Tamil also figures as an official language.

Another policy decision felt by the Tamil as discrimination against them was the "policy of standardization" adopted in 1971 by the government of President Sirimavo Bandaranaike. This policy was intended to have the effect of reducing the proportion of Tamil students at the university level to make room for candidates from educationally underdeveloped districts.

Discrimination is also enshrined in the constitution of the country. It enjoins on the Republic to „give to Buddhism the foremost place", and to note that „accordingly, it shall be the duty of the State to protect and foster the Buddha Sasana".[14] As we know, the Tamil in Sri Lanka are Hindu by religion. Actually, both sides, the Tamil and the Sinhalese, who are mostly Buddhist, have used religious emotions in election campaigns. Even monks were not above taking sides in politics.

9. Caste Conflicts in Hindu India

In India too, discrimination among Hindus based on the caste-system is going strong. When progressive sections of the educated elite held sway in politics, they took reform measures, similar to "affirmative actions" in the USA, for ameliorating the situation of the downtrodden castes. But there was much resistance to such actions from high-caste Hindus – for instance, violent demonstrations against reservations of university places for students from the lower castes (in the 1990s). Today, with Hindu-nationalist and conservative politicians in power since 2014, high caste Hindu publics are forcing the country back to the oppressive atmosphere of the past.

In India, the caste system of Hindu society has always been also a strong political factor. Not only the main four castes – the *Brahmans, Kshatriyas, Vaishyas, and Shudras* (priests, warriors, traders, and workers respectively) –, but also the various sub-castes in each of these four and the numerous lower "scheduled" castes and tribes have made the Indian jungle of identities and politics more complicated than in any other country.

Division of a society in *castes* (as distinct from *classes*) is not altogether unique to Indian Hindus. The system exists in some form or other in some other societies too. Only, there it is not so strongly fixed by some religious code, as in Hindu India. It exists(ed) in Sub-Saharan Western African countries (Senegal e.g.) and in Spanish and Portuguese colonial societies in South America (*sociedad de castas*). De facto, caste divisions exist also among Indian Muslims and Indian Christians. Among the former, there are said to exist three castes: *Ashrafs* (nobles), middle caste Muslims called *Ajlafs*, and the lowest, the *Arzals*, are equivalents of the lowest castes among the Hindus. Among the Indian Christians, there are some who identify themselves as *"Brahmin Christians"* and some whom others identify as *Dalit* (downtrodden) Christians. The system's existence in different societies up to our times makes me think that there must be some *general* reason for its origin, and continued existence other than just cultural backwardness of the country and society.

The *basic behavioral characteristics* of us humans have remained largely similar for the greater part of our social evolution. (according to Desmond Morris in *The Naked Ape*). Since we are social animals, we want to and need to – like chimps – *belong to a group* – a family, an extended family, or some larger group or community. This group gives each of us our collective *identity*. Belonging to our group has always been very important for both material help, economic security and psychological stability. Especially in poor, underdeveloped countries or regions, tribal/ethnic identities and corresponding loyalties help a lot.

In India, it is often the caste identity that helps. It is often the influence of senior caste-members that e.g., helps a young person find a job. And it also helps in elections if the candidate belongs to the right caste. Some high caste-identities – e.g., Brahmin or Kshastriya among Hindus – bring also *social prestige and power*, for which all humans have a weakness. It is easy to understand why people who possess such hereditary "higher" identities, privileges, and related power mostly also want to preserve and flaunt them.

It is also easy to understand the resentment of those who neither like their inherited low caste identity that others gave their forefathers, which may not at all be related any more to their current profession, nor possess any additional higher identity (e.g., businessman), nor have a chance to attain some. They are no longer willing to tolerate the hereditary privileges of the higher castes, nor their own hereditary sufferings and disadvantages. In India, for this reason, since many years now, frequent caste conflicts break out, and they often turn violent.

10. Language-Identity and Language-Nationalism as Factors

Bangladesh

Like religion, the mother tongue of a person is a very strong identity. Above, I have given the example of Mujibur Rahman, leader of the liberation movement of Bangladesh. The Bangladeshis of today were until 1971 East Pakistanis. Around 1947, on the eve of independence of the Indian subcontinent, the majority of those who lived in Eastern Bengal, being Muslims, opted for the soon to be created state of Pakistan, a homeland for the Muslims of the Indian subcontinent. But there was also a proposal to form a third state, the state of Bengal comprising all the Bangla speaking regions of India.

Two decades later, East Bengali Muslims realized that they had made a great mistake. Although they constituted the majority of the population of Pakistan, those who effectively governed the country were West Pakistanis, especially the Generals and their military. The Bengalis from East Pakistan were very much underrepresented in both the armed forces and the central administration. And the surplus that resulted from export of rice and jute products from East Pakistan were used for paying the imports of West Pakistanis.

What was worse, West Pakistanis could not tolerate that East Pakistanis continued to speak and write their mother tongue *Bangla*, the high form of which had been developed by Hindus who lived mainly in West Bengal, a province of India. The central authorities dominated by Urdu speaking West Pakistanis banned broadcasting Bengali literature and music, including the works of Rabindranath Thakur, the great poet of all Bengalis. They also tried to impose Urdu as the only state language. Such policies led East Pakistanis to feel that their province had been reduced to the status of a colony of West Pakistan. The Bengalis of East Pakistan reacted with the *Bangla Language Movement*, as a result of which the central government was compelled to introduce Bangla as the second state language.

I cannot here narrate the whole history of Bangladesh. Suffice it to say that in the liberation movement of the country (1970 – 1971), discrimination of their mother tongue *Bangla* was the strongest causal factor, though, no doubt, economic and political discrimination, as everywhere, played a role too.

India: Some Cases from Recent History

Also in India, the multiplicity of well-developed Indian languages and peoples speaking these as mother tongue have given rise to language-related ethnic feelings. However, fortunately, no ethnic group except the Sikhs, who speak Punjabi, tried to secede. That may be partly ascribed to the fact that, despite India's large expanse and huge population, the educated middle class everywhere has accepted English as their *lingua franca* and one of India's official languages. But some conflicts could not be avoided. Let me describe a few cases.

Hindi (rather various regional colloquial versions of High Hindi) is, generally speaking, the mother tongue of most Indians in Central North India. During the independence movement, it was tacitly assumed that after the end of British rule, English could not remain the language of the central government. In the Hindi-speaking regions it was similarly assumed that Hindi would be declared to be the national and official language of India. But that was not to be. When Hindi-speaking leaders in the capital New Delhi, situated in central North India, tried to implement this change, it was brusquely rejected in the whole of South India with its Dravidian languages and Dravidian cultural tradition. One could see there graffiti such as *"Hindi never, English ever."* And other regions too opposed the introduction of Hindi as the national language and the sole official language of the central government. The situation today is that „There is no national language of India as per the constitution, Hindi and English both are considered the official languages of India."[15]

Apart from this, beginning in the early 1950s, several times, constituent states of the federal Republic of India had to be reorganized because of language conflicts. Bigger states were divided up into smaller ones, and so it went on even after 1956, when the whole country was divided up and reorganized in smaller states on the basis of the language spoken by the majority of the people of the parts. In some cases, following the same principle, even bigger districts, were divided up and the two parts were attached to two neighboring states. It also needs to be stated, however, that at least in four cases, also religion played a role: in case of Meghalaya (74% Christian), Mizoram (87% Christian), Nagaland (88% Christian), and Punjab (58% Sikhs).[16]

In India, in some cases, mother tongue as collective identity played a nasty role in struggles between communities of Indians over land, jobs, and small business opportunities. It manifested itself in the far Eastern province (federal state) of *Assam*. There, 48.4 % of the population speak Assamese, but a sizable minority, 28.9 %, speak Bangla, and 6.7 % speak Hindi.[17] Most members of the two minority communities have been living there since long. But many others, both Hindus and Muslims, had immigrated from Bangla-speaking West-Bengal and Bangladesh after 1971, when Bangladesh came into being, and settled down there. Such immigration into Assam had begun in the period of British rule over hundred years ago and continued into our times. As everywhere else in India, among Assam's original Assamese-speaking population too there have been many Muslims, who had converted into Islam in the previous centuries. In 2011, the total share of the Muslim population in Assam was 34.22 percent.[18]

In such a state, the population grew from 8 million in 1951 to 31 million in 2011. It was estimated to have been 35 million in 2018.[19] At the same time, as for the area of the province, Assam became much smaller since 1956 due to states reorganization (see above). When economic growth could not keep pace with population growth and growth of aspirations of the people, troubles began. Assamese speaking people, the original inhabitants of the province, have been complaining since long that people from the other provinces of India and Bangladesh – also labelled as *aliens* – were legally and illegally immigrating into Assam and occupying jobs, business opportunities, and arable forest land, which, they said, should go to the Assamese, the sons of the soil. To make matters more complicated, in the past few decades, the number and percentage of Muslims, who had for a few centuries now constituted a substantial minority of Assam, have been swelling because of illegal immigration of Bangla-speaking Muslims from Bangladesh, thus also fanning the already existing Hindu-Muslim conflicts in the province.

Riots, often murderous, aimed at large-scale displacement of Bangla-speaking people had already begun in the late 1950s and continued to take place off and on. All these troubles culminated in a long-time effort of the Indian state to find out who among the population of Assam were not really citizens of India, but illegal immigrants from Bangladesh. They were to be deported at the end of the process. That is a long and complicated story, that need not be narrated here.[20]

More such examples could be given from India. In the past (late 1960s), *Maharastrians*, sons of the soil in *Maharastra* (in Western India) – economically the most highly developed province (state) of India – started a sort of campaign to protest against immigration of too many South Indians, who were allegedly occupying too many white-collar jobs, for which legitimately locals should have been recruited. About a decade or so later, they expressed the same sort of opposition to the appointment of too many *Biharis* (from the province of *Bihar* in eastern India) in menial jobs.

A very recent example is the campaign of *Tamils*, – sons of the soil in *Tamilnadu*, a province (state) in southern India – against immigration from North India into their now well-developed state, in which many new industries are coming up. Moreover, many of them are nowadays saying that „India is not at all one nation but [a] union of states and so Hindi cannot be the national language." The leader of a newly founded extremist nationalist state party – "We Tamils Party" – has demanded of the state government „exclusion and expulsion of non-Tamils, especially Hindi speaking people, from Tamil Nadu" (Victus 2023).

11. Separatism in The Western World: Belgium, Quebec, Catalonia, Scotland, Yugoslavia

Language identity and language nationalism seem to be universal phenomena. Their strength can also be observed in the Western World. As examples, I shall here give short reviews on five such cases.

Belgium: three language regions

Belgium as a state is purely a product of European history, of the various wars and competitions for influence between duchies, monarchies, empires etc. It took its present stable shape only in 1830.

Because of such an origin, the country comprises three language-regions: Wallonia (French speaking), Flanders

(Dutch-, or Flemish-speaking), and bilingual Brussels. From the beginning until in the recent past, French has been its only official language, also for the Flemish-speaking people. Flemish, as the language of "Dutch speaking" Flanders, used to be sneered at as the language of peasants. There has also been an economic reason behind it. French speaking Wallonia was the region where industrialization of the country started and made rapid progress.

Like the Bangla-speaking people in East Pakistan, the Flemish-speaking people did not tolerate it for long. A sort of antagonism developed between the two language groups, and it still exists.

This ongoing antagonism led since the 1970s to far-reaching reforms, which changed the formerly unitary Belgian state into a federal one consisting of the aforesaid three language-based regions. Since then, the Belgian political landscape has become a difficult terrain, making government building after an election a long difficult process. It is now also a culturally divided country. To illustrate the division, there are two Green Parties in the small country: *Agalev*, the Flemish Green Party, and *Ecolo*, the French one.

Quebec

Quebec, Catalonia, and Scotland – regions/provinces of Canada, Spain, and the United Kingdom respectively with varying degrees of autonomy and devolution of power – are trying for several decades now to free themselves from their present status and become fully independent states.

Quebec was a French colony (called New France), but, for various reasons, weaker than the British colonies further South (New England). In several Anglo-French wars (1759 – 1763), England prevailed and New France became a British colony. But assimilation or even integration of the French-speaking settlers failed to materialize.

Beginning in the 1960s, there has been a rise of Quebec nationalism with the founding of a new militant political party called *Front de Liberation du Québec* (FLQ) devoted to achieving independence of the province. Between 1963 and 1970 they perpetrated many acts of violence, e.g., bomb attacks and bank raids. One ruling politician was kidnapped and later found murdered. Their final goal was to create a Marxist-communist state in Québec. The government responded by passing a War Measures Act that allowed incarceration without trial. The FLQ was ultimately subdued.

As against that, another party, *Parti Québécois*, tried to achieve independence through peaceful means. They came to power in the province in 1976 by winning the election and held a referendum in 1980 on the issue of independence. But the majority of the inhabitants of the province (59.5%) rejected independence – obviously out of economic considerations. In October 1995, a second referendum for Quebec sovereignty was held. It too was rejected, but by a slim margin (50.58% "No", 49.42% "Yes").[21] The central government was accused of using unfair means to influence the result.

The movement, however, has had some success. Today, Quebec enjoys the status of a "nation" in the Federation of

Canada, which is much more than just an autonomous region. And one of the important purposes of the movement, namely to raise the status of the French language, has also been achieved. French was already, since 1977, the official language of Quebec. In 2022, the provincial legislature passed a law, called „*Act respecting French, the Official and Common Language of Quebec*".

Catalan nationalism

Catalonia was for a long time in its history a sovereign principality. It lost its independence in 1714 after the surrender of Catalan forces in the War of Spanish Succession.

During the Second Republic (1931 – 1939) the region enjoyed self-government and the language again became the official language of the region. But after the defeat of the Republic, during the Franco dictatorship, it lost both.

Catalonia was an industrialized region of Spain. During the Franco dictatorship it suffered economically. But recovery started around the beginning of the 1960s and the region again became prosperous. And then under the constitution of the new (monarchical) democracy (1978) Catalonia regained self-government, albeit only in internal matters.

But many Catalans were not satisfied with mere autonomy in internal affairs. They wanted to regain independence. Already in 1931, their leaders had demanded the status of a republic within Spain, but had finally accepted autonomy.

Certain negative developments in the economic and political spheres – the economic crisis following the finance crash of 2008 and the ruling of the Constitutional Court in 2010 that declared certain parts of the Autonomy Statute of 2006 unconstitutional – sparked off huge protests. Around 2010, there was a resurgence of Catalan nationalism. Since then, calls for independence became louder and more frequent.

For independence, Catalans have done everything they could short of waging a liberation war, but till now to no avail. They have held two elections to the regional parliament – in 2012 and 2015 – and two referenda on self-determination. The result of the first, non-binding, referendum held in 2014 was a large majority for self-determination. But because the anti-independence voters had boycotted it, the turnout was too low to be convincing. In 2015, a new – this time binding – referendum was called. But the Centre banned it on legal grounds. The regional government defied the Centre's ban and held it in 2017. But the Centre prevented smooth voting by applying brutal police violence and arresting pro-independence leaders. Nevertheless, the Catalan regional parliament passed a resolution proclaiming Catalonia's independence. But it was nullified by the Centre, which at the same time took control of Catalan institutions. The president of the region and five former cabinet ministers had to flee the country.[22]

Scotland

In Scotland's history, there have been several conflicts between the royal dynasties of Scotland and England, the latter trying to conquer the territory or occupy the throne of the former.[23] And there has also been fighting back on the part of the former.

In the second half of the 12th century, Scotland was reduced to the status of a vassal kingdom of England. In 1296, Scotland had to recognize the king of England as "overlord" (suzerain). But there were also resistance and uprisings. One reads of two Wars of Scottish Independence, which ended in 1357 with a treaty through which Scotland regained its independence.

In the following centuries, after a checkered history of wars and battles, and competition for succession to the thrones of Scotland and England, the two kingdoms were united in 1707 through the *Act of Union* that brought into existence the Kingdom of Great Britain.

This time the Scots, at least the great majority of the ruling classes, gladly agreed to lose their sovereignty, for economic reasons: (1) Toward the end of the 17th century, Scotland was suffering from a slump in trade, (2) four years of bad harvests (1695 to 1699) that caused famine and depopulation, and (3) the disastrous failure of a project to establish a Scottish colony in the Isthmus of Panama, because of which the investors, including the middle class of Scotland, lost a huge lot of money, and the kingdom stood on the brink of bankruptcy. (4) All this was happening while England was moving toward becoming a strong imperial power and profiting from this development through expanding trade.

The union was a good decision for Scotland. It lost its independence, but England saved Scotland from bankruptcy by taking over the financial obligations resulting from the failure of the colony project in Panama. The long-term benefits that Scotland enjoyed from the union were manifold: (1) As part of a super-power of those days, Scotland, formerly a poor agricultural country, also profited from growing trade. Scots in general became wealthier. (2) The underclass, who were earlier used to being oppressed by the aristocracy, could now breathe more freely. (3) And last but not least, thanks to the union, the spirit of enlightenment entered Scotland.

All these advantages and benefits notwithstanding, the spirit of independence resurfaced in Scotland in recent decades. Scots are after all a distinct ethnic group, have a distinct history, and Scottish is a distinct language, although *today*, 98 % of the people of Scotland speak English (30 % speak also Scottish).

And, as is the case ever so often, there were also some immediate economic grounds for the rebirth of the independence idea. Decline of the fishing industry (partly due to EU membership of the UK) and deindustrialization in the wake of globalization played a role. But the most important economic factor was the discovery of large oil deposits in the North Sea off the East coast of Scotland. 90 % of the oil fields would be located in Scottish territorial waters if Scotland were an independent state. But as things were then, all the oil revenues went to the union budget, i.e., budget of the government of Great Britain. Scottish nationalist politicians thought it was Scotland's oil and Scots were being deprived of revenues from their wealth.

They might also have been thinking that – after the decline of the superpower Great Britain since the end of the

Second World War – the economic and other material advantages and benefits of union with England that they once enjoyed, could also be had by an independent Scotland through its membership of the European Union.

To make a long story short, there arose a movement for Scottish independence, and in 2014, the devolved Scottish government held, with the consent of the union government, a referendum on the issue among the residents of Scotland. But the majority, 55.3 %, of those who voted (84.6 % of the registered voters) said at that time No to independence.[24]

Striving for independence has, however, not come to an end. Now that the UK has exited from the EU, Scotland shares with England many disadvantages in international trade. Scottish nationalists are demanding a second referendum on independence.

The Tragedy of Yugoslavia

The most complex of all cases of separatism has been the case of the former *Socialist Federal Republic of Yugoslavia*. This country had been built upon the ruins of two empires that expired at the end of the First World War: the Austro-Hungarian and the Turkish Ottoman empire.

The core of this new state-creation was the Kingdom Serbia. Its career began as the principality of Serbia that existed in the early 19th century, but was under the suzerainty of the Ottoman Empire. Because of its decline, the latter withdrew its troops from Belgrade in 1867. Since then, the principality enjoyed de facto independence. In the aftermath of the Russian victory over the Ottomans

(1878), Serbia attained full independence, and in 1882, the European powers elevated its status to that of a kingdom.

In the Balkan region, each of those peoples who later formed the country called Yugoslavia have had two identities: One was "race"-based. They all understood themselves as "Southern Slavs" ("Yugoslavs"). The other was their ethno-cultural identity, based on language. These peoples, depending on their mother tongue, identified themselves also as Serbs or Croats or Slovenes, etc. What is worse, a third factor, viz. religious affiliation, co-determined their second identity. Croats and Slovenes have been mostly Catholic Christians, Serbs Orthodox Christians. In Kosovo, which was an autonomous province in the Serbian Republic, ca. 95 percent of the population have been (are) Muslims. In North-Macedonia, Muslims make up about 32 percent of the population, Orthodox Christians 46 percent.[25]

Ethnicity and religion got combined to become a strong factor of conflict: That was particularly the case in Bosnia-Herzogovina. There, before breakout of the war, almost half of the population (43.7 %) were Bosniaks (Muslims), 31.4 % Serbs (Christian Orthodix) and 17.3 % Croats (Catholic).[26] They even wrote in different alphabets: Latin and Cyrillic (as the Serbs)[27].

In the good old days of the Socialist Federal Republic, the state and the members of the Communist Party succeeded in minimizing the importance of religion in social life. But when later the disintegration of the Republic began, religion gained in importance as an identity-giving factor. Ethnicity and religion got combined to become a strong factor of conflict: Croat and Slovene Catholics stood opposed to Orthodox Christian Serbs. In Kosovo, Muslim Kosovars violently opposed the dominance of Serbs, whereas in *Krajina*, a region of Croatia, its Serbian majority declared independence and vainly tried to join the Republic of Serbia. In both regions, in the 1990s, many brutalities were perpetrated by both sides.

The above-mentioned factors and their combinations, of course, played very important roles both in the creation of Yugoslavia and in the conflicts. They generally aroused strong emotions, and were therefore most talked about. But here too, as always, the factor economic interests played perhaps the most important, though a silent, role.

After a long period of strong economic growth, the Yugoslav economy suffered a serious setback in the 1980s. It was due to the two oil price shocks of 1973 and 1979 that caused a world-wide economic crisis, under which Yugoslavia too suffered.

The country's economic growth had been based on foreign debts and export-oriented investments, and it depended on the same policy more heavily in order to come out of the crisis. But it failed. In the two years 1989 and 1990, over 600,000 workers were made redundant, and half a million more were not paid wages, in order to save their companies from bankruptcy. Over one thousand enterprises were liquidated.[28] All this happened in a supposedly socialist country under the rule of a communist party, previously unimaginable. The united republic of Southern Slavs began to fall apart.

Misha Glenny, journalist and famous Yugoslavia specialist of those days, reported the following from a conversation with economics Professor Mate Babic of the University of Zagreb and former Vice-Premier of Croatia:

„Yugoslavia was founded [...] as a political imperative – without any consideration for the economic needs of the region. In the socialist federation of the post-war period, the imbalance between the Slovenian level of civilization and the developing-country status of Kosovo could only be corrected through massive state control over the economy. This caused resentment in the prosperous North, the fruits of productivity of which was transferred to the dusty climate of the South, where they rotted in the sun. Additionally, a deep distrust arose between Slovenia and Croatia on the one side, where a tradition of zealous work ethic ruled, and Serbia on the other, situated as it had been for long close to the border of the Ottoman empire with its corrupt economic standards. To be tied, for better or for worse, to the Serbian economy contained a harmful long-term effect on the economy of Slovenia and Croatia. When the political decay of Yugoslavia accelerated in the republics, the economic tensions resulted in the deepening of distrust." (Glenny 1993: p. 107. This is not a direct quote from the conversation between Glenny and Matic, but only a paraphrasing done by Glenny himself).

The "political imperative" had consisted in the desire of Croat and Slovene nationalists of the early 20th century to free themselves from the hegemony of Austro-Hungarians and Italians by uniting with the other Southern Slavs, particularly with Serbia.

12. International Collective Identities

Being Woman as a Collective Identity

Women everywhere have taken cognizance of the fact that the *average man* of their collective is taller, more muscular, physically stronger, and so more suited to do heavy work than the *average woman*. They therefore accepted, or rather put up with, men as natural leaders in big-game hunting, in warfare, and so also in societal matters – also because they themselves were almost permanently busy with pregnancy and child rearing. "Evolution-God" made it so. Anthropologists may have found evidence of matriarchy in some ancient societies, but patriarchy was the norm.

With the advent of modern industrial civilization, the importance of muscle power and ability to do hard work diminished. Parallel to this, for women, also the burden of multiple pregnancies and child rearing diminished. This made it possible for women to do things that had hitherto almost exclusively been men's work: ploughing the field, going to factory or office for earning money for oneself and/or the family. It also made possible for women to go to high school, study in the university, do research, start a business, even join the armed forces. This was possible because, unlike size of the body, physical strength and muscle power, intelligence and intellectual ability was distributed by "Evolution God" equally between men and women.

This cultural change led to another: Women no longer accepted as natural the dominating position of men in society, nor the domineering behavior of husbands and fathers in the family. The Women's Movement was born. But it was mainly born in rich countries, where women could fairly easily fend for themselves, and where a system of social welfare payments existed.

The above brief review shows, I hope, that the rise of the women's movement is a function of technological development followed by resulting socio-economic and cultural developments. In underdeveloped countries, it is limited only to the higher echelons of society.

In highly developed countries, emancipation of women led to a conflict situation between men and women, as if between two collective identity groups. The number of divorces started rising. The number of births per woman began falling. Having a child began being talked about as a poverty-factor. In many rich countries, the state started paying a child allowance. In Germany, I once read a report naming ten childless young women who said they wanted to have a child, but could not find a suitable willing male partner. Today, such societies are becoming "aging societies". Industries are lacking in trained young workers.

All this, taken together, should be called a conflict between desire for individual freedom, for living according to one's interests and ambitions, on the one hand, and the interests and requirements of society at large. Who will work for paying us our pensions? That is a major worry of the older generations. But the women's liberation movement as a whole promotes and supports such an individualistic conception of emancipation from patriarchy.

This has however been criticized by socialist-feminist women, who maintain that women's emancipation can never be complete as long as society is not emancipated from capitalism, for capitalism is patriarchal.

Today, for prestigious and/or highly paid jobs in politics, administration, and economy, women do not only compete as individuals. Very often, they raise demands as a *collective identity group*. In many countries, women are clamoring for a certain *quota for women* in such jobs. In Germany, e.g., a women's quota in management boards of big companies is being demanded. Particularly in politics, since all parties must also woo women voters, who constitute half of the electorate, it has become very easy to put this demand through. Such things *naturally* breed bad blood between the two sexes.

Being woman as a collective identity could and should *logically* encompass women of all countries. Logically, in analogy to the socialist and communist Internationals of the working-class movement, there should have been a Feminist Women's International. But none has been there, none exists. What exists is merely the slogan "In Sisterhood", and that is an empty slogan, as empty as the slogan "Workers of the world, unite."

Black People's Collective Identity

Ancestors of those blacks, who today live in the western hemisphere, had been abducted and transported as slaves to the plantations of white people. But even today, long after liberation of their grandparents and great grandparents from slavery, in the USA and some Latin American countries, such as Brazil, where the Whites rule, Blacks' social and economic status is de facto that of second-class citizens. Even though some Blacks of these countries could climb up the socio-economic ladder, they, on the whole, remained the underclass. In the US, the police and other security people kill black citizens regularly just on the basis of some suspicion, and often get away with it. Not even a black professor can escape suspicion of being a burglar when he enters his house in a professors' quarters zone of a university campus through the side door. (I saw in the TV a report on this incident.)

They tried to overcome such a status by means of various political actions, such as demonstrations and slogans like "Black is beautiful" and "Black lives matter". Many tried to acquire a new identity by converting to Islam and formed a *Nation of Islam.* Some others tried the same by founding a new religion, namely Rastafari[29] (worshipping Haile Selassie, onetime Emperor of Ethiopia, as living God and Messiah). Or they founded a militant political group and called it *Black Panthers.* All that did not help much. Except in the areas of sports and modern music, they, in their majority, could not become equals of Whites.

The point here is that Blacks in these countries understand themselves and are seen as a *collective identity group,* a disadvantaged minority to boot, needing special attention and "affirmative action".

The Blacks in the USA may be a special case. But the ancestors of Blacks in Sub-Saharan African States were not slaves. They, of course, suffered under European colonial rule, partly also under North African Arab rule. But after independence was achieved in the 1960s, they have been led by their own black leaders or chiefs. Nevertheless, in the international arena, they, the people in general, are in reality looked down upon (particularly in Europe these days) because of the unending stream of illegal and unwelcome immigrants.

In the destination countries of Europe, into which the immigrants gatecrash, the majority of the local populations are having the feeling of being invaded by an unarmed army of illegal immigrants, against whom they must defend themselves, but do not know how.

When I came to Germany as a student, that was in 1964, I experienced a similar looking down upon the Indian people, because India was in those days known as a bitterly poor, famine-stricken, country. I often had to hear the question: why you Indians do not eat the meat of the stray cows on your streets? Or a question like: Don't you Indians and Pakistanis have better things to do than making war? Neither Indians nor Pakistanis are on average black, they are brown. Nor was there in those days a stream of illegal migrants from South Asia to Europe. It is this experience that gave rise to my thesis (mentioned above) that a person who is a foreigner in Europe and North America receives a treatment proportionate to the per capita GDP of his native country.

Notes and References (Chapter 4)

1. American author Samuel Huntington has written a book with the title *Who are We?* (Huntington 2004).

2. I have read about these things in: Irenäus Eibl-Eibesfeldt (1984) and William Catton (1980). They also used the related terms "pseudo species" and "quasi species" (see also chapter 3).

3. For a definition of the terms ethnie, ethnicity or ethnic group see note 1 at the end of chapter 3.

Definition of the term „tribe":

Tribe (history, anthropology): An ethnic group larger than a band or clan (and which may contain clans) but smaller than a nation (and which in turn may be contained within a nation). The tribe is often the basis of ethnic identity. (https://en.wiktionary.org/wiki/tribe, accessed: 11.5.2024)

Tribes are therefore considered to be a political unit formed from an organisation of families (including clans and lineages) based on social or ideological solidarity. Membership of a tribe may be understood as being based on factors such as kinship ("clan"), ethnicity ("race"), language, dwelling place, political group, religious beliefs, oral tradition and/or cultural practices. (https://en.wikipedia.org/wiki/Tribe, accessed: 11.5.2024)

4. https://www.shortform.com/blog/zulu-and-xhosa-rivalry/ (accessed: 7.5.2024)

5. Integration does not demand that one completely gives up one's own cultural origin (religion, mother tongue, mores and customs). That would be assimilation, i.e., complete adaptation to the society of the majority, while losing the language and culture of one's country of origin.

6. For more details on the conflict in Manipur see Sadokpam (2023) and Sarkar (2023).

7. Manipur Census data, https://www.census2011.co.in/census/state/manipur.html (accessed: 11.5.2024); https://de.wikipedia.org/wiki/Manipur#Demografie (accessed: 11.5.2024)

8. https://de.wikipedia.org/wiki/Malaysia#Bevölkerung (accessed: 11.5.2024)

9. But the "Boat-People" from Vietnam were not only saved from drowning, they were also brought to Germany and given asylum / were adopted. All organized and carried out by Cap Anamour, a German voluntary organization. Why this difference? My view: That was in the second half of the 1970s, and the Boat-People were "victims of communism". Saving them from communism was felt to be a noble thing to do.
That is another, though indirect, confirmation of my thesis that the respect (or lack of it) a personally unknown foreigner gets is proportional to the per capita GDP of his native state. The average Arab from an oil-rich Gulf state is brown; and he is treated with much respect.

10. http://notesonpakistan.blogspot.de/2009/08/two-nation-theory.html (accessed: 7.5.2024)

11. https://www.frontierweekly.com/articles/vol-54/54-27/54-27-Pot%20Calling%20the%20Kettle%20Black.html (accessed: 11.5.2024)

12. https://de.wikipedia.org/wiki/Sri_Lanka#Demografie (accessed: 5.5.2024)

13. https://en.wikipedia.org/wiki/Sri_Lanka#Contemporary_history, https://theconversation.com/sri-lanka-has-a-history-of-conflict-but-the-recent-attacks-appear-different-115815 (accessed: 5.5.2024)

14. https://en.wikipedia.org/wiki/Sri_Lanka#Religion (accessed: 5.5.2024)

15. https://currentaffairs.adda247.com/national-languages-of-india/ (accessed: 7.5.2024)

16. „Understanding Religious Minorities in India: Key Characteristics and Recognition", https://himalayanexpress.in/2023/06/01/understanding-religious-minorities-in-india-key-characteristics-and-recognition/ (accessed: 8.5.2024)

17. https://de.wikipedia.org/wiki/Assam#Sprachen (accessed: 8.5.2024)

18. https://de.wikipedia.org/wiki/Assam#Religionen (accessed: 8.5.2024)

19. Assam's population from 1951 to 2011: https://de.wikipedia.org/wiki/Assam#Bevölkerungsentwicklung; population estimation 2018: https://www.quora.com/How-many-people-are-there-in-the-state-of-Assam (accessed: 8.5.2024)

20. For more information on the situation in Assam see Gobain (2018) and Sharma (2018).

21. https://de.wikipedia.org/wiki/Québec#Separatismus (accessed: 9.5.2024)

22. https://en.wikipedia.org/wiki/Catalonia#Independence_movement (accessed: 20.5.2024)

23. On Sottish history see e.g. https://de.wikipedia.org/wiki/Geschichte_Schottlands, https://en.wikipedia.org/wiki/History_of_Scotland, https://en.wikipedia.org/wiki/Scottish_independence (accessed: 21.5.2024)

24. https://en.wikipedia.org/wiki/2014_Scottish_independence_referendum (accessed: 20.5.2024)

25. For figures on the distribution of religious denominations in Kosvo and North Macedonia see: https://de.wikipedia.org/wiki/Kosovo#Religion (accessed: 21.5.2024); https://en.

wikipedia.org/wiki/North_Macedonia#Religion (accessed: 21.5. 2024).

26. https://de.wikipedia.org/wiki/Bosnienkrieg#Bevölkerungs-struktur (accessed: 21.5.2024)

27. Serbian is written using both the Latin and Cyrillic alphabets. The Cyrillic alphabet has been the standard in the Constitution of the Republic of Serbia since 2006. In reality, however, all Serbs are proficient in both alphabets and texts and printed matter are sometimes written in one script and sometimes in the other. (https://www.grammatiken.de/serbische-grammatik-online-lernen/serbische-schrift-kyrillische-buchstaben-aehnlich-latei-nisches-alphabet-aussprache-anders.php, accessed: 21.5.2024)

28. https://en.wikipedia.org/wiki/Yugoslavia#Ethnic_tensions_and_economic_crisis (accessed: 9.5.2024)

29. Rastafari: The main features of this faith are recognizing Haile Selassie as the Reincarnation of Messias and Living God on Earth, rejection of the Western political system (which it calls Babylon or Babylon-system and considers to be corrupt and discrminating). Its followers also struggle for equal rights of the Blacks.   (https://de.wikipedia.org/wiki/Rastafari#Bewegung, translated by S. Sarkar)

Chapter 5

Conclusions

Conditions of Peace

In his *A Study of War*, Quincy Wright (1965: 100) wrote a sort of a summary of the history of civilization:

> „Out of the warlike peoples arose civilization, while the peaceful collectors and hunters were driven to the ends of the earth, where they are gradually being exterminated or absorbed, with only the dubious satisfaction of observing the nations which had wielded war so effectively to destroy them and to become great, now victimized by their own instruments." (quoted in Wilson 1978/1995: 116)

But such are the facts; we are all living in civilization, even most of the tribal peoples of the world.

Against the background of all the knowledge on wars and conflicts presented in the foregoing chapters, we can now talk about conditions of peace in our world.

We can generalize that *economic interests* have been the strongest, though not the only, factor in the history of conflicts and wars among humans and among groups of humans. The will to survive and to pursue one's own economic and other material interests related to survival (i.e., selfishness) was ingrained in our character, when we evolved from some ape species. That is what the theory of evolution says. But it has not been an absolutely dominant trait of our character, not in all situations. Primatologists who have studied character traits of chimpanzees, our closest relatives in the animal world, have come to a conclusion that agrees with everyday observations of us humans made also by ordinary people. Eminent primatologist Frans de Waal (2006: 136) writes:

> "Both humans and chimps are gentle, or at least restrained, toward members of their own group, yet both can be monsters to those on the outside. I am simplifying of course, because chimps can also kill within their own community, as can people. But the in-group versus out-group distinction is fundamental when it comes to love and hate."

When it comes to love and hate, powerful emotions can be aroused and conflicts with out-groups can lead to violence, even to war. Only the borders between the in-groups (sometimes aka Identity groups) and the corresponding out-groups have never been stable in the course of history.

With reference to the biblical commandment „Thou shall not kill", Irenäus Eibl-Eibesfeldt writes:

> „The interesting question is however whether we declare our support for this article of faith only on the basis of rationality, or whether we additionally also follow innate proclivities. If the latter is the case, then our hope for peaceful co-existence would surely be better founded than if only compulsion or pure reason makes us law-abiding." (Eibl-Eibesfeldt 1971: 113, translated by S. Sarkar)

De Waal thinks we may have this hope. Even lay people know and can observe that we humans, like animals, have some genetically inherited inhibitions that control aggression, particularly inhibition to kill members of in-groups. More such innate tendencies can be observed among our nearest relatives, the chimpanzees. De Waal found that chimps share with us humans character traits like generosity as well as a sense of morality. He writes in his books (1996, 2006, 2010) that the human character traits empathy, kindness, helpfulness, solidarity and cooperation must also be innate, because they are not uniquely human, they are also present in apes.

Also Eibl-Eibesfeldt, who, with Konrad Lorenz, believes in the existence of an innate aggression-drive in humans, cannot be regarded as a complete pessimist. He writes, let me repeat, in an essay (1990: 81, translated by S. Sarkar):

„We are not fully predetermined by our instincts. We are capable of controlling our nature through culture. [...] What is decisive is that we are the first creatures that can set goals for themselves and thus give our life a meaning. By doing this, we, of course, do not free ourselves from [our] nature. But we actively enter into new situations, in which new conditions of selection act upon us."

It is not clear in this quote how, according to Eibl-Eibesfeldt, the new conditions of selection would act upon us. Will they act in the usual biological evolutionary way? That is, through genetic mutations and selection of those mutants that are best adapted to the new requirements of the changed situations?

Ian Morris, a famous historian of the genre Big History, of course accepts the ethological thesis of presence of innate aggression in humans, but, unlike Eibl-Eibesfeldt, he does not think that assumption of a special ability to make radical cultural adaptations to new situations is necessary for hoping that in some near future, say in the next 30 to 40 years, peace will be possible (Morris 2014).

Morris thinks that although war is a terrible thing, on the whole, the wars of the past have also brought progress, technological as well as political, albeit inadvertently. Things that were invented as weapons and/or further developed in order to get some advantage in war, later also proved to be valuable for civil life. Sooner or later, all peoples of the world copied the inventions. Thus, a competition for ever better inventions and innovations arose among rival powers, which drove technological progress ahead for the whole human civilization.

After every war, when peace came, ever increasing trade between formerly enemy countries (and also others) enriched societies of both. And trade required better law and order, better administrations and many other better institutions. Even if one people was defeated and integrated in the kingdom or empire of the victors, the defeated and subjugated people also contributed to the might of the victors and hence had also to be granted the advantages of living in a large and strong state/empire.

This essay is not the right place for a detailed summary of Ian Morris' book (*War! What it is Good For?*). Suffice it to say that Morris thinks that the horrendous costs of war and the great advantages of peaceful co-existence are so obvious that soon making war would become obsolete, an anachronism.

There is also not enough space here for a detailed critique of all the points that Morris makes for his argument. I shall here mention only the *basic flaw* in it. Morris has arrived at his conclusion by studying the development of human civilization through the past centuries. And he assumes that in the foreseeable future our civilization would go on developing in the same manner and in the same direction. He assumes continuous economic growth and incessant political progress. His hope (prognosis, if you will) of a peaceful world in the near future totally depends on these two assumptions. His book appeared in 2014.

The same flaw in thinking builds the basis of the expectation of a *"demographic dividend"* in certain newly rising developing countries such as India, where population growth has been continuing in the current decades. I remember having heard such talks even from India's leading politicians. The reasoning was that a plethora of cheap laborers contribute to industrial development of hitherto underdeveloped countries.

But the Club of Rome's famous book *Limits to Growth* (by Meadows et al.) appeared already in 1972. This possibility, that there are limits to growth, cannot be ignored. After all, all essential nonrenewable resources that our civilization needs, including arable land, are limited, and it is becoming ever more difficult and ever more expensive to extract them. Also, the capacity of nature to absorb man-made pollutions is limited. Otherwise, there would not be any necessity to raise such alarms as we hear since many years now. Parallel to this, the global human population is growing continuously, albeit at a slower rate than before.

Eibl-Eibesfeldt, in the quote above, does not indicate what "new situations" he is thinking of. So far as I can visualize, those would be the dire consequences of climate change, and of other global and local environmental damages. Shortage of essential resources may lead to resource wars. It is already causing large-scale unwelcome immigration from overpopulated countries into the rich countries. Technological solutions to such problems are increasingly becoming difficult, if not impossible. This is a completely new political-economic situation.

Thinkers like De Waal and Eibl-Eibesfeldt appear to have thought about the problems of war and peace in isolation. They thought about these, of course, in connection with the results of their own scientific research on human and animal nature. But they, like Morris, appear to have been working under the assumption that in the surrounding areas of human life, other things and developments would remain more or less the same, or, when changes take place, the direction of the changes would remain the same, i.e., ever better and upward. They did not notice, it seems, that in the areas of economic, political and social conditions, and in the related areas of thought, massive changes have been taking place that should necessitate a whole shift from the hitherto valid "Growth Paradigm" to what I call "Limits-to-Growth Paradigm" (Sarkar 1999).

Thinkers, who have accepted this paradigm shift seriously, already know of the possibility of world-wide economic, political and societal collapse. They are writing books on subjects that, taken together, may be called collapsology.

Now let us suppose that in such a new situation, the leaders of the world are in a position and have the strength to take the right decisions and set the right short-, middle- and long-term goals, for the world as a whole as well as for their own particular countries. So far as I can reasonably see, these decisions would have to be such that they would initiate a worldwide economic contraction, *degrowth* in modern jargon. Mankind must accept these goals and adapt itself to everything resulting from implementation of the corresponding policies. That would be a collection of radical cultural, economic, and political changes. That would not happen through a gradual millennia-long process of spontaneous genetic mutations and selections. And if the needed changes do not take place very soon, the world would sink into global chaos with dozens, if not hundreds of low-intensity wars, civil wars and conflicts – big and small. The wars and conflicts of the future would not be waged for building empires, but for defending "our" land, or for taking possession of the land of "others", and, for that matter, the mines containing valuable minerals. Already now, we can see walls and fences being erected at many places between sovereign countries and territories. The wars in Palestine-Israel have always been about possession of land. Similar has been the case in

Rwanda (Diessenbacher 1998). And in Western Sahara, the bone of contention are the phosphate mines.

But science-savvy people may ask: can't we use genetic engineering for solving once for all the problem of peace? John Keegan (2012: 133), a military historian, tried to imagine a biological-evolutionary solution to the problem of innate aggression, that leads to frequent wars and other acts of violence: He writes:

> „A successful adaptation through mutation, in whichever way the latter may have occurred, is a reaction to the *conditions of the environment*. Although […] genetic engineering may make it possible to bring about ‚specific mutations' or ‚genetic mutations' and thus breed creatures without any aggression, it would be necessary for their survival to keep them under conditions in which there would be no threat for them. But such conditions do not exist in the natural environment, and they cannot also be created. Even if a fully agression-free human race would come into being and would live under exclusively favorable circumstances, it would still see itself compelled to kill; apart from lower organisms (germs) that cause diseases and insects and tiny animals that house the disease-germs, also bigger animals that compete with humans for plants, on which the latter subsist. One can hardly imagine how creatures that are incapable of any kind of aggressive reaction would be able to control their environment." (translation and italics by S. Sarkar)

Prospects of peace have become very dim. A long period of (violent) conflicts and societal collapse in one country after another is in the offing. It seems to me, if we at all dare to speculate on a peaceful world, then it should be temporally located after the long era of collapse, during which the world population will go down drastically. We already know enough about the factors of wars and conflicts. This knowledge only needs to be spread.

If government leaders want to do something for peace already before that time, they can enforce a birth control policy in countries where population is still growing. A non-growing population would immediately lead to increase in per capita availability of all consumption goods. And that would, incidentally, also mitigate the severity of the other causes of conflict, such as unemployment and illegal migration. De Waal writes:

> „We know that bonobos presently live in a richer habitat than chimps, one that allows mixed groups of males and females to forage together. This permits greater social cohesion than in chimps, who in their quest for food split up into small parties. The 'sisterhood' among unrelated females that is typical of bonobo society would not have been possible without predictable, abundant food sources" (de Waal 2006: 227f.)

Another thing that should be done, but is very difficult to do, is to drive out from the head of young people the thought that the task of their governments and political parties is to make them ever more prosperous and happier. The primary task of governments today is to save the environment for life in general, including animal life. But to achieve any degree of success in this direction, a degree of egalitarianism must become part of the core of policy.

If cultural leaders of a society want to, dare to, try to contribute something toward peace, they can try by all non-aggressive, non-offending and non-provocative means to reduce the importance of a person's religious and other similar identities. What exactly should and could be done in this regard is a discussion that must be carried out, but at another place.

Literature

Barash, David P. (2013): *„Are We Hard-Wired for War?"*, in: New York Times, 28.09.2013

Bartlett, Robert (1993): *The Making of Europe: Conquest, Colonization and Cultural Change 950 – 1350*. London (Penguin)

Catton, William R. Jr. (1980): *Overshoot – The Ecological Basis of Revolutionary Change*. Urbana etc. (University of Illinois Press)

Deschner, Karlheinz (ed.) (1990): *Woran ich glaube*. Gütersloh (Gütersloher Verlagshaus)

De Waal, Frans (1996): *Good Natured. The Origins of Right and Wrong in Humans and Other Animals*. Cambridge MA, London (Harvard University Press)

De Waal, Frans (2006): *Our Inner Ape – The Best and Worst of Human Nature*. London (Granta Books)

De Waal, Frans (2010): *The Age of Empathy: Nature's Lessons for a Kinder Society*. London (Souvenir Press)

Diamond, Jared (1998): *Arm und Reich – Die Schicksale menschlicher Gesellschaften*. Frankfurt a. M. (Büchergilde Gutenberg)

Diamond, Jared (2006): *Collapse – How societies choose to fail or survive*. London (Penguin)

Diessenbacher, Hartmut (1998): *Kriege der Zukunft –Die Bevölkerungsexplosion gefährdet den Frieden*. München, Wien (Hanser)

Eibl-Eibesfeldt, Irenäus (1971): *Liebe und Hass – Zur Naturgeschichte elementarer Verhaltensweisen*. Frankfurt a. M. etc. (Büchergilde Gutenberg)

Eibl-Eibesfeldt, Irenäus (1984): *Krieg und Frieden – aus der Sicht der Verhaltensforschung*. Munich, Zurich (Piper)

Eibl-Eibesfeldt, Irenäus (1990): „*Glaube als Offenbarungswissen und Zuversicht*", in: Deschner (1990)

Emcke, Carolin (2010): *Kollektive Identitäten – sozialphilosophische Grundlagen*. Frankfurt, New York (Campus Verlag)

Frederickson, George M. (2002): *Racism – A short History*. Princeton, NJ (Princeton University Press)

Freud, Sigmund (1933): *Warum Krieg? Pourquoi la guerre? Why War?*. Herausgegeben vom Institut für geistige Zusammenarbeit am Völkerbund. Paris 1933: Correspondence; ‚Open Letters. Bd. 2, 25-62

Einsteins Brief: in: Freud (1933), 13-27 (Erstveröffentlichung)

Fromm, Erich (1973): *The Anatomy of Human Destructiveness*. New York (Holt, Rinehart and Winston)

Fromm, Erich (1974/1994): *Anatomie der menschlichen Destruktivität*. Reinbek (Rowohlt)

Gide, Charles et al (1953): *A History of Economic Doctrines*. London etc. (George G. Harrap)

Glenny, Misha (1993): *Jugoslawien – Der Krieg, der nach Europa kam*. München (Knaur Taschenbuch)

Gohain, Hirain (2018): „*An Open Letter to Indians*", http://frontierweekly.com/articles/vol-51/51-7/51-7-An%20Open%20Letter%20to%20Indians.html (accessed: 19.5.2024)

Guibernau, Montserrat and John Rex (1997): *The Ethnicity Reader*. Cambridge (UK) (Polity Press)

Huntington, Samuel (2004): *Who are We? – Die Krise der Amerikanischen Identität*. Hamburg, Wien (Europaverlag)

Kaiser, August (1973): *"Aggressivität als anthropologisches Problem"*, in: Plack (1973)

Keegan, John (2012): *Die Kultur des Krieges*. Köln: (Anaconda Verlag)

Keeley, Lawrence H. (1997): *War Before Civilization*. New York, Oxford (Oxford University Press)

Lorenz, Konrad (1966): *On Aggression*. London (Harcourt, Brace & World)

Lorenz, Konrad (1963/1985): *Das sogenannte Böse*. München (dtv Verlag)

Meadows, Donella, et al. (1972): *Limits to Growth*. New York (Universe Books)

Meller, Harald & Schefzik, Michael (ed.) (2015): *Krieg – eine archäologische Spurensuche*. Halle (Landesamt für Denkmalpflege und Archäologie)

Morris, Desmond (1967/1994): *The Naked Ape*. London (Vintage Books)

Morris, Ian (2010): *Why the West Rules – For Now*. London (Profile Books)

Morris, Ian (2014): *War! What it is Good For? The Role of Conflict in Civilisation, from Primates to Robotes*. London (Profile Books)

Pinker, Steven (2011): *The Better Angels of Our Nature*. New York (Viking)

Plack Arno (ed.) (1973): *Der Mythos vom Aggressionstrieb*. Munich (List Verlag)

Priester, Karin (2003): *Rassismus – eine Sozialgeschichte*. Leipzig (Reclam Verlag)

Rattner, Joseph (1995): *Klassiker der Psychoanalyse*. Weinheim (Psychologie VerlagsUnion)

Sadokpam, Dhiren A. (2023): „*What is really behind the vio-lence in Manipur?*", https://frontline.thehindu.com/news/what-is-really-behind-the-violence-in-mani-pur/article66820969.ece?cx_testId=25&cx_testVariant=cx_1&cx_artPos=0#cxrecs_s (accessed: 19.5.2024)

Sahlins, Marshall (1974): *Stone Age Economics:* London (Routledge), reprint from the first edition (1972)

Sahlins, Marshall (1960): „*The Origin of Society*", Sci. Amer. 203 (3)

Sarkar, Saral (1999): *Eco-Socialism or Eco-Capitalism? – A Critical Analysis of Humanity's Fundamental Choices.* London (Zed Books)

Sarkar, Saurav (2023): „*The Ethnic Violence in Manipur, India, Explained*", https://countercurrents.org/2023/09/the-ethnic-vio-lence-in-manipur-india-explained/ (accessed: 19.5.2024)

Sarrazin, Thilo (2010): *Deutschland schafft sich ab. Wie wir unser Land aufs Spiel setzen.* München (DVA), 2nd edition 2012

Schriefl, Ernst (2021): *Öko-Bilanz – Wo wir stehen, was zu tun wäre, wohin wir steuern.* Norderstedt (Books on Demand)

Sharma, Devabrata (2018): „*Assam – Contextualising NRC Historically*", http://frontierweekly.com/articles/vol-51/51-7/51-7-Assam%20-%20Contextualising%20NRC%20Histori-cally.html (accessed: 19.5.2024)

Smith, Anthony D. (1997): „*Structure and Persistence of Ethnie*", in: Guibernau and Rex (1997)

Ullrich, Otto (1979): *Weltniveau – In der Sackgasse des Industriesystems.* Berlin (Rotbuch)

Literature

Victus, Solomon (2023): „*Recent Discourses on Tamil Nationalism*", https://frontierweekly.com/articles/vol-56/56-16/56-16-Recent%20Discourses%20on%20Tamil%20Nationalism.html (accessed: 11.5.2024)

Wallace-Wells, David (2019): *The Uninhabitable Earth – Life After Warming*. New York (Tim Duggan)

Weber, Max (1997) „*What is an ethnic group?*", in: Guibernau and Rex (1997)

Wilson, Edward O. (1978): *On Human Nature*. Cambridge MA (Harvard University Press)

Wrangham, Richard & Peterson, Dale (1996/2001): *Bruder Affe – Menschenaffen und die Ursprünge menschlicher Gewalt*. Kreuzlingen (Diederichs)

Wright, Quincy (1965): *A Study of War*. 2nd edition, Chicago (University of Chicago Press)

About the Author

Saral Sarkar was born in 1936 in a village of West Bengal, India. After graduating from the University of Calcutta (Kolkata), he studied German language and literature for five years at the Goethe Institute in India and Germany. From 1966 to 1981, he was lecturer of German at the Goethe Institute in Hyderabad, India.

Since 1982, he has been living in Cologne, Germany, where he has been active in the Green Movement, Anti-Globalization Movement, and all kinds of ecological and leftist movements. He was member of the Green Party of Germany from 1982 to 1987, but left the party in deep disappointment.

Over the years, Sarkar has taken part in many discussions and debates in the above-mentioned areas and published widely in political journals in India, Europe, and the American Continent. His basal theoretical work *Eco-Socialism or Eco-Capitalism? A Critical Analysis of Humanity's Fundamental Choices* (1999, London) has also been published in German, French (in internet), Chinese and Japanese.

His other major works are: *Green-Alternative Politics in West Germany, Vol. I & II* (1993, 1994, Tokyo), *The Crises of Capitalism – A Different Study of Political Economy* (2012, Berkeley), which was originally published in German

(2010, Neu-Ulm), the two volumes of *Eco-Socialism or "Green" Capitalism? Collected Writings of Saral Sarkar* (2023, Norderstedt) and *Was ist Ökosozialimus?* (2024, Marburg).